Published by Boulevard Books.
First edition 2015.
Reset
Germer, Fawn.
Library of Congress Control Number: 2014920126
Copyright © 2015 By Fawn Germer

Other titles by Fawn Germer:
Hard Won Wisdom, Perigee Books, 2001
Mustang Sallies, Perigee Books, 2004
Mermaid Mambo, Newhouse Books, 2007
The NEW Woman Rules, Network Books, 2007
Finding the UP in the Downturn, Newhouse Books, 2009
The Ah-Hah! Moment, Strauss Books, 2010
Pearls, Newhouse Books, 2012

Boulevard Books is a division of Strauss International
Printed in China by Four Colour Print Group, Louisville, Kentucky
ISBN 9780983877219

Cover and interior design by Barbara Willard

www.fawngermer.com
Speaking information: info@fawngermer.com (727) 467-0202

WORK-LIFE
Reset

BY
FAWN GERMER

BOULEVARD
BOOKS

To today, because I love you.

ACKNOWLEDGMENTS

I can't imagine doing a book without my A-team of Barb Willard on design and Lynn Stratton on editing. These two pros have been with me for years and work so hard to make me look good. And I am thrilled to welcome editor Lori Draft to the A-team.

Thanks to Carrie Snyder for her copy edits and to Kate Brassfield, who edited the magazine article I wrote on my beach reset and helped me to clarify my vision for this book.

Thank you to my friends — the true-blue, there-in-the-darkest-moments friends — who held me up when I had trouble standing in the shadow of grief and loss. I am also grateful for my beaches at Honeymoon and Caladesi Islands, the trails in Hammock Park, the clear waters of the Weeki Wachee River, and the sun, because they also healed me. Not to mention my dog, Louie, and my four cats, Katie, Little Bit, Cubby, and Evil Willy.

Thanks to my mom and dad — for everything. I recently realized that my mother is the answer that is always inside of me when I don't know what to do. My father is the knowledge that there is always hope. Always.

Finally, thanks to my best friend and partner, Julie Hipp, who waited. I am so lucky — and I know it.

CONTENTS

INTRODUCTION
RESETTING

Your computer slows down. Like, waaaaay down. It's bad. One false move and you know you will lose everything you've been working on for days, so you keep trying to make it work in its diminished state. But it doesn't get better.

It gets slower.

You have no choice.

You reboot.

Voila! It purrs back to life like a brand new computer! All you did was restart it. And somehow, it dumped its baggage, cleaned out the sludge, and now the motherboard is humming happily along.

Wouldn't it be great if you could reset yourself like that? Dump your baggage and take out the emotional garbage that's slowing you down?

Whether you're in a depression or you're facing a life that is terribly out of balance, a reset can be your miracle turning point. It's you deciding that enough is enough. It's you taking the power that you either didn't know or forgot that you had.

A reset is not a do-over. It's a start-over. It is a conscious and deliberate choice to take charge and do what calls your soul — giving it a good jolt. A reset.

It won't allow you to bypass your pain completely, but it can definitely minimize it and put you in charge again.

We reset ourselves all the time. There's the annual life reset, New Year's, when we officially turn the page. There's the diet reset, which usually happens on a Monday. The exercise reset usually begins with an amazing burst of commitment that often fades quickly. We make commitments to overhaul our job performance, our ambitions, our work-life balance, our community work.

We start things over all the time.

If you want to do a reset on January 1, have at it. And if you want to do it on January 14, have at it. Just do it.

I want to lead you to a path beyond our routine resets (*"I'll start dieting on Monday"*), a path to a far more dramatic and life-changing reboot that involves a conscious choice on a soul level, a path to mark the end of one way of living and the beginning of another.

We'll explore the specifics later in the book, when I share how I dropped everything and hiked 70 miles on pristine beaches to force-quit the worst personal tsunami I'd ever experienced. That is an example of what I call a "hard reset." And, let me tell you something — it was a personal intervention that changed me forever. If you need a hard reset, it'll be up to you to design it. I'll help you with that.

You can reset your life by juicing for a month or going vegan or eating boiled peanuts.

You can reset at a yoga retreat or spa or a religious tent.

In Honolulu or Nairobi or Paris or Peoria or in your basement.

You can do it filling your days with people you love,

people you haven't had time for, people who enlighten you, people who make you laugh — or you can let go of people who no longer fulfill your needs.

You can do it by following old familiar paths or by choosing roads you have never traveled (or imagined).

You can reset by decluttering your house. Or redecorating. Or moving.

Maybe you will sit on an island, a boat, on top of a mountain, in a cave, by a campfire, on a dock, in a teepee, beside a river. Go shark fishing for a week, or grouper fishing.

You could float in the middle of a lake or swim from one end to the other. Raft the Grand Canyon, attend a weeklong bridge conference, try 20 new recipes.

Climb the stairs in a tall building. Bungee jump from a bridge. Go skydiving, hang gliding, cliff diving, SCUBA diving.

Hike the Appalachian Trail. Rent a Harley. Visit 20 New Orleans jazz clubs, or 15 clubs that play the blues in Memphis.

Have a reading marathon. Or a writing marathon. Or spend two days calling all your old friends. Or a week in silence.

A week away from your partner. A week without electronics.

Twenty-four hours of prayer. Forty-eight hours of prayer. Two weeks of prayer.

This reset list is endless. Endless.

What should you do to reset? Don't ask me. It's all about you. What matters to *you*?

How long does your reset take? It takes as long as it takes. A day, a week, a month. You'll know.

And you may not need to do anything extraordinary.

It all depends on you. Sometimes you don't have to do anything but make up your mind.

But other times it requires more effort, and you have to take action to gain the clarity and space to make it happen. You may find that lucidity through meditation and prayer, a body cleanse, music, athletics, camaraderie, travel, cooking, walking across hot coals, or anything that liberates your soul from your routine.

What matters most is the conscious decision to end one chapter and begin another by deliberately memorializing the occasion.

I've heard the story of a man who used a tattoo of the words "I'M DONE" to commemorate his reset. He had the word "I'M" tattooed on the inside of his right upper arm. On the left, the word "DONE" was tattooed. He would flex his arms in the mirror and say loudly, "I'M DONE."

Because he was.

Are you?

Author Cheryl Strayed famously hiked 1,100 miles on the Pacific Crest trail as a reset after her mom died. And no one illustrated this idea better than Forrest Gump, the fictional character who was of below average intelligence but brilliant in his wisdom. In one pivotal moment, he sat on his front porch, broken-hearted.

He stood up, stepped off the porch, and started running.

"That day, for no particular reason, I decided to go for a little run..." He ran to the road, then decided to run to the end of town, then across the county. By that point, he decided, "Maybe I'd just run across the great state of Alabama..." He kept running — for three years. Eventually, he was swarmed by reporters and fans, none of whom could "…believe somebody would do all that running for no particular reason."

He told the reporters, "I just felt like running."

Obviously, there was a reason he felt like running. He'd had enough. He was done.

Running let him move out from under his pain. Was he running away from something or going deep within, the only way he could? Either way, it gave him time and space to process his feelings, and it gave him control over his life. His past was behind him, not because he'd run away from it, but because he had taken the step to graduate out of it.

"My Momma always said you got to put the past behind you before you can move on. And I think that's what my running was all about." All told, Forrest said he ran for three years, two months, fourteen days and sixteen hours.

And after all that running, he just stopped one day, right in the middle of Monument Valley.

He was done.

He'd moved on.

He'd reset.

CHOOSING RESET

When I Googled "life reset," I found myself drowning in a bunch of garbage from self-anointed life coaches who have a 30-day plan, a workbook, a weekly newsletter, blah, blah, blah that will help you live a magnificent life for a hefty fee.

That's snake oil.

Reset begins and ends inside of you, and you don't

have to pay for some wizard to tell you what your heart is more than willing to reveal.

You don't need a guru, a coach, a program, or anyone standing over you directing you. What you need is the determination to make the reset happen.

It is one of the most personal decisions you will ever make, and it's my hope that this book will give you the courage to make it.

Reset is not just a mini life overhaul. You don't reset your entire equilibrium by deciding to lose ten pounds, or switch jobs, or give up drinking, or get a divorce. A reset begins with a huge change in your psyche that requires planning, execution, and commitment.

When a computer reboots, it (hopefully) goes back to the place in time when it worked. That reset makes the old system purr again by just giving it a moment to collect itself and start over.

If you are in the throes of serious clinical depression, try a reset — but don't do it without also getting professional help. Why not use every possible lifeline? You don't get extra points in life for stubbornly living it the hard way.

When a person reboots, he or she stops, takes account, and then restarts, fresh and hopeful.

INVITING CHANGE

I reset after my worst year ever. My mom and dad died in my arms less than three months apart. My seven-year relationship fell apart. I was betrayed by one of my very best friends. And it seemed like every week there was some other crisis I had to face. As the year's anniversary of my mom's death passed, I realized I had to do something.

For months, I'd considered taking antidepressants. I'd used them 20 years earlier when I got divorced. I certainly don't judge anyone who uses them. But I'd resisted doing that through my grief because I really believed that, as I'd grown, I'd developed the coping skills that would get me through any depression without medication. My formula was prayer + affirmations + exercise + massive quantities of fresh air in the great outdoors.

It had always worked for me, but it wasn't enough for my worst year.

"Well, are you going to give it another year?" I asked myself. "Because if you do, it could be like this for the rest of your life. You either need to get some medication or you need to *do* something."

I had to do something.

I was going to do something.

As I contemplated how to invite change into my life, I realized that I needed to get back to *me*. I didn't want to turn into a different person. I liked who I was. I just didn't know where I'd gone. I missed my old self. I wanted to be back in my skin, where I laughed easily and felt a constant rush of gratitude and joy by just waking up and walking my dog. Was that part of me gone forever? It sure felt like it.

In my reset moment, I chose to walk 70 miles of beach, much of it deserted.

Imagine my surprise when, just a few days after I hit bottom, I found my old self again. On the fourth day of my beach walk, I felt hope. I started looking forward to what was in front of me. It was that easy. I went from darkness to light that fast, all because I stopped to reboot.

Reset is all about taking back the power you've lost, whether it was due to adversity or personal resignation. Reset is reclaiming your energy, joy, verve, hope, direction, and essence.

Defibrillator paddles are designed to send a shocking jolt through the body, resetting the heart and filling you with life. A reset experience can do the same thing.

But for all of us, reset is a way to take charge of yourself, whether you need to reset your life balance, your work, your mindset, your boundaries, or your body.

It may seem like you need a big, complicated answer to your big, complicated problem. But maybe the answer is really something small and simple.

You may just need to reset.

CHAPTER 1

IT'S TIME

In the end, there were about twenty photos on the wall beside my Uncle Chuck's bed. He was 89, and he was failing.

He didn't bring a lifetime of possessions with him when it was time to go to the home. Just his bed, his chair and his photos. Every night, he'd look at the photographs, one at a time.

"These are all the people in my life," he told me. "There's Teddy in high school. Oh, this one, this one is really precious to me. There's Mom, there's Aunt Ev... Over here, here's your dear mom and dad. I love that picture..."

It went on for more than ten minutes. Every day, every night. When he finished, he would say a prayer of gratitude as he looked at his cherished photos. That dear man taught me so much during his lifetime, but his final lesson was the most important.

When all is said and done, all we have are those photos on the wall and the memories they represent.

It won't matter what we did for a living or what we earned or what kind of house we lived in or how far we traveled. What will matter is who we were to other people, and how much love we shared.

That is the real business we are carrying out on this earth. It's easy to get sucked into the importance of business and career and money and things, but we are here to love and be loved. We are here to be the best human version of ourselves that we can possibly manifest.

When I'm speaking onstage, I'll often use a Power-Point slide of an old movie still of a woman on her deathbed. She says, "Okay, I only have a few more minutes, so let's review the budget for the next fiscal year..."

Everybody always laughs at it because what kind of a nut-pot would think of something so meaningless on his or her deathbed?

Yet we sacrifice so many days in our young, healthy years obsessing about things that, in the end, won't matter at all.

Are you spending your time on what matters most?

If not, reset.

Of course, we all have certain obligations that we have to fulfill in order to live the lives we want to live. But these are secondary to what is really important in life. You can enjoy your work, you can enjoy your possessions, but look at your life by looking at your day. When you reach the end of the day, ask yourself if there was any newness to it, any learning, any love, any energy, any movement.

So many people don't get that clarity until it's too late to do anything about it. You can decide to have that awareness right now.

TIME WARP

We warp our perspective in a number of ways. We get trapped thinking about the past, we worry about the future, we obsess about expectations, we give too much importance to our jobs and the drama of the workplace, and we let the media tell us what's going on instead of figuring it out for ourselves.

We sort of stumble through life instead of taking control and making conscious daily decisions to live a full life. While we are living it, life seems to present a confusing menu of intrigue, challenge, and drama.

This all seems to change as we near the end. In our final moments, the fog lifts and the confusion clears. There is nothing left to prioritize. We are done with our things because we can't take them with us. Our power and position are useless. There is nothing left to see or do because time runs out when it runs out.

If we didn't fill our lives with what brought us joy, oh well. Everything on our to-do list either got done or it didn't, but again, oh well. Our plans die with us.

Once we are out of here, it won't matter what we owned, what we won, or how thin and beautiful we were. None of those concerns move on with us.

> "My favorite things in life don't cost any money. It's really clear that the most precious resource we all have is time."
>
> – *Steve Jobs*
>
> "Never get so busy making a living that you forget to make a life."
>
> – *Unknown*

I've read a number of essays and books that ask the question, what would you do if you had just 10 or 30 or 90 days left to live? What if we didn't wait until we had only 10 or 30 or 90 days left? What if we didn't wait until we were old to think that way? What if we reset and truly lived TODAY?

You should live just as large when you have thousands of days left. And if you aren't doing that, then it's time to reset so you do.

WHAT WILL YOU DO WITH TODAY?

By midnight tonight, you will have spent another of your priceless, limited days on this earth. Hope you are doing something incredible with it.

The average woman in the United States lives to be 82.2 years old — or 32,193 days. The average man lives to be 77.4 years old — or 28,251 days. By the time you're 25, you have spent 8,760 of your days. To see how many days you have left (assuming you are average), take your current age and multiply it by 365. Then subtract it from the total for your gender.

As of today, I've lived 19,639 days. I've lived an extraordinarily full and happy life, but I know that, sadly, I have lost thousands of days because I either wasn't paying attention or I outright sacrificed them because I was swamped with obligations. I try hard to avoid that now and to make each day count. To stop at some point, take a deep breath, and just "be." To do something that makes the day unique and special. It's not that hard. Even if it's claiming just 10 minutes to make a day spectacular, I do that.

Because you know what? I don't really know how many days I have left.

I did the math and know, that if I am average, I've got 12,554 days in front of me. Maybe more, maybe less. But I don't really know.

Hopefully, you have many, many, *many* days in front of you. But you just don't know. I have lost enough friends to automobile crashes and cancer to know that our timelines are very unpredictable. You don't get a certified letter or an e-mail or even a text telling you when your time is coming. But it *is* coming. Maybe tomorrow, or maybe when you are 100. Nothing is certain.

All you know for sure is what you have right now.

The only certainty is today.

So don't be so quick to lose a day because you're busy with your routine. You don't have to live like that, so why would you choose to?

I recently had a conference call with a senior executive who wanted me to help his beleaguered workforce be less stressed about the lack of balance in their lives. Sixty- and seventy-hour weeks were not uncommon. They do important work, but the company has fiscal issues and the workload is going to get worse — not better.

His people are angry and frustrated. Many have quit. Others are thinking about it. Recruiting, training, and replacing them is expensive.

So what is this leader's solution?

Hiring me, a speaker specializing in work-life balance! Ludicrous.

As if any speaker can talk for an hour or two and

placate thousands of people who are angry that they have no lives. That shows how out of touch the guy is.

"Don't say, 'Work less, enjoy more.' Just tell them what they *can* do, given that each of them is doing the jobs of three people," he said.

Wow.

What could I possibly say that would heal someone who is exhausted from routinely working stress-filled, 60-hour workweeks? Someone who is feeling stuck in a situation that is causing them to neglect family, church, community, and self in the process?

My heart hurt for those people.

It shows how an oppressive workplace will steal your life from you *if you let it.*

You do have options. You may not be able to exercise them immediately, but you cannot be imprisoned by anyone but yourself.

Sure, you can invoke the traditional work-life balance tricks that create more time in your calendar. You can focus. You can embrace the concept of owning and managing your calendar. But unless you're in a situation where you are valued as a human being, you can't even start to achieve balance or honor your "choices" in life.

IS IT WORTH IT?

If you are working for a company that regularly demands you put your home life last, you need to go somewhere that gives your mind clarity and ask yourself these questions:

1. What are you sacrificing to work there?
2. What are you gaining?

3. Is what you are gaining worth what you are sacrificing?
4. How long are you willing to make the sacrifice?
5. Why are you really working there?
6. What will it take to get out of there?
7. What are you waiting for?

This issue is not limited to abusive work situations. It is the same for a relationship that is depleting your soul, rather than filling it with life. A whole lot of us have stayed in relationships that should have ended sooner. If you are in that kind of a situation now, ask yourself these questions:

1. What are you sacrificing to be in that relationship?
2. What are you gaining?
3. Is what you are gaining worth what you are sacrificing?
4. How long are you willing to make the sacrifice?
5. Why are you really staying in the relationship?
6. What will it take to get out of it?
7. What are you waiting for?

It's exactly the same issue, whether you are being sucked under by a job or a bad relationship. It is all too easy to surrender your power and your precious time because change is uncomfortable. Change upsets other people. It is never easy, and the outcome is rarely clear. And those who are in these kinds of situations are often so worn down they think they will not get hired elsewhere or find someone else to love them.

You can find another job.

Someone else will love you.

The future is as bright as you allow it to be. It's yours, and it is for you to design, either by intention or by default.

So ask yourself: Are you taking charge of your life, or are you wasting time?

Really?

Consuming jobs and careers exist, and if those feed your soul, then embrace them. Enjoy them. You are free to make that choice, and I support your freedom to work as hard and long as you want. If it's stressful, but you enjoy the stress, then don't change a thing. Do whatever it is that fulfills you and makes you happy — as long as you are not hurting other people.

But if you are sacrificing your most precious, perishable gift in life — time — to something that is depleting your soul and robbing you of purpose, then you need to stop right where you are, ask yourself what you are doing, and start making changes.

Every single day has the potential for joy, happiness, challenge, and greatness. You get 365 chances each year to have a great day. Even the happiest people get a few bad ones, but if you aren't having great days most of the time, you've got to ask yourself why, and then ask what you are going to do about it.

How much time are you going to waste?

It's easy to latch onto a set of priorities for the wrong reasons. You can live the way you think you are "supposed" to live, acquire the things that are "supposed" to matter, and build your legacy on values others have taught you are "supposed" to count.

But this life isn't about other people and their definitions of what is important. It's your life. And remember, you only have today.

It's time.

How long are you willing to endure a work or relationship situation that is keeping you from going deep and truly developing who you are on a soul level? Because there are plenty of companies and legions of "leaders" who will take everything you've got and leave nothing for you. There are plenty of significant others who will suck the life out of your significance.

When you devote yourself to the wrong person, company, cause, or path, you lose a hell of a lot more than your energy and brilliance. You lose something you will never get back: your very limited time.

IT'S NOT TOO LATE

Once it hits you that your days are moving faster and your time is getting shorter, you really begin to examine the choices you've made in the past. So fill your days with delight now, rather than experiencing loss or regret when it hits you that time is running out.

The older you get, the harder it is to change jobs or find new relationships. It's certainly not impossible, but stop making excuses and start taking charge now.

Do not throw your time away.

Work life and non-work life usually don't balance out so well. We have 168 hours to live each week. At a minimum, you are probably working 40 hours. Add in five hours for lunch. Five hours for getting ready for the day. At least five hours for commuting. Most people sleep at least seven hours a night, so that's 111 hours of your week just sleeping and getting yourself off to work – if you're not working overtime.

That leaves you with 57 hours to use as you wish.

Shocking, huh?

Now add in your overtime. Count the time you spend with the family, reading to the kids, cleaning, cooking, lawn care, financial management, household management. Grocery shopping, going to school plays and soccer games and taking the car to the shop, going to the doctor, checking in on your parents, and going to your house of worship. Maybe some working out, too. And time for Facebook or other social media, and for reading something.

Even with all of that, you'd think there would be time to actually breathe in some life and do things that you love.

But where is it?

If you're waiting for things to slow down once the kids get a little older, or for the merger or system upgrade or new management change to finally settle things down at work, you are sacrificing the only sure thing you've got in this life: today.

Take a few minutes and think about what will matter once you reach the end of your days. What you will cherish then is what you should cherish now.

What matters are the people you love, the people who love you, the places you've been, the moments that brought you joy and meaning and life.

It's all about the pictures on the wall.

CHAPTER 2

THE 'GET A LIFE' RESET

If you wake up knowing that today is going to wind up looking the same as yesterday — and you're tired of it — *do something*. Get out of your rut.

A reset is a fantastic tool for climbing out of darkness, but it is also the only tool for balancing a lopsided life. You can try to tweak this or that in an effort to achieve some sort of life harmony, but a reset marks the beginning of the new life you are claiming for yourself.

Is it time?

Do you feel guilty because you don't have the time to be there for the people who love or need you? Frustrated because you don't have ten minutes to yourself? Foggy because your brain is stretched so thin that you have little to offer in terms of creativity or humor?

Reset.

Do you need to call in sick just to catch your breath? Have you been ignoring your physical health? Do you have a huge bucket list of the things you really want to do someday? Do you use all of your vacation? Do you use it to do the things you enjoy most? Do you work while you are on vacation?

Well, good grief. Reset.

Do you work for people who are so demanding it's

hard to have a life and a career? Are you so personally consumed by work that you sacrifice time with your loved ones to do things for work? Are you envious of people who manage to have both a life and a career?

Take back your life. *Reset.*

Are you checking your work e-mails when you go home at night? More than once? More than twice? More than three times?

Knock it off! *Reset.*

Is your life lacking meaning and purpose? Are you honoring your values with your time, or sacrificing your time to things you don't really value?

Well, guess what?

NO MORE WAITING

Today you are one day closer to your death. You don't get a do-over on life, so make the choice to live right now.

You deserve a harmonious, fun, full life filled with adventure and love, challenge and purpose. But if you are like so many people caught up in the crazy demands of an insanely paced world, you aren't in balance.

I don't really like the word "balance" because life teeters all the time between our different callings. Still, "work-life balance" remains the catch-phrase for people who want to successfully work and have a life, so I use the term.

Life is always a little out of whack. The stars do not align themselves to make things nice and easy for you. Sometimes it's as if the universe is deliberately throwing too much at you.

As if it is forcing you to choose.

It's not about balance. It's about choices.

CHOOSE WHO YOU WANT TO BE

Who are you?

On the inside.

Who?

Do you think about that much? Enough? Is the soul inside of you freed or suffocated by the choices you've been making about how you spend your time?

You have the same number of hours each week as everybody else. How you spend them is up to you. You own your time. There are sacrifices for every reward.

You choose whether you want to work more and earn more. You choose if you'd rather work less and play more. You choose who you are going to pair up with. You decide how educated you are going to be. You control so much about how well you take care of your body.

Granted, many early choices impact what's ahead for you. I once wrote an article about a woman who had six — SIX! — children by age 22, when her husband bolted. She didn't have the luxury of thinking about life harmony and "me time," so she'd likely find a book like this useless. So would many parents with newborns or small children.

But fortunately, many of us have the ability to make changes in our lives and decisions about what we want — a huge luxury when you think of those people who have no choices at all.

Choosing not to make the choices that honor what calls you is denying your precious personal freedom. Pay attention to what is going on in your life, and take responsibility for the choices you are making.

Change is not going to happen if you don't make it

happen. Everything is right in front of you, yet you may be like so many others who hesitate, afraid their whole world will unravel if they dare to make the choice to live in a way that honors their true priorities.

It is so easy to lose a year or two years or a decade because you lack the courage to take full responsibility for the time you have. But why do that? Do you think the problem is going to fix itself overnight if you don't do anything to make that happen?

All you have to do is choose.

I got into a friendly verbal tussle with Domenique Camacho Moran, a very influential lawyer in New York, regarding women who leave the practice of law to create balance for their families right before they make partner.

She stated that such life choices — in law and in the corporate world — are destroying opportunities for other women to work in an environment where they have the same representation in partnership and the C-suite that they had in their graduating classes. She's sick of being one of three women in a room with 45 men, and I get that.

"It is a sacrifice for those who stay," she said. "Making it all work here at work and at home is the hardest thing I do every day. But if I don't do this, my daughter will never be at the partnership table or in a C-suite where women are represented in the same numbers that existed in her graduating class."

Again, I get that.

The argument hits at core values. Her core values are just as worthy as anyone else's, but what matters to her can't trump what matters to others who might not share her values. Fresh out of law school, women join firms in the same proportion as men. But by the time they're up for partnership, most of them are gone.

A 2014 report by the American Bar Association shows that more than 45 percent of associates (who do not hold any ownership of their firms) are female, but fewer than 20 percent of partners (who do have ownership) are women. Worse, women represent just four percent of the managing partners in the 200 largest firms in America.

Why? The hours, the politics, inequities in pay, sexist environments... The list goes on. And they make choices to stay at home, too.

Domenique is right. It'll never get better if women keep leaving.

If their main goal is making history (which is not a bad thing), women should make that sacrifice. But I don't think we can judge anyone for choosing not to be miserable, stressed, or away from their children. That choice to leave and stay home is just as worthy as the choice to be a superstar lawyer.

The choice to leave to do anything that fulfills your self is perfectly valid. I got a rise out of Domenique when I said I'd leave the firm to have more time for kayaking.

There is no right or wrong answer in this. It all depends on whose life we are talking about. Where are you in this debate?

LIVE NOW, NOT LATER

"That is beautiful," I said.

The last time I'd seen Anne Johnson, she and her husband had quit their jobs to sail the world. Two decades later, we reconnected on her back patio, and she showed me a picture of herself jumping from a huge rock into a pristine mountain lake.

"Not a care in the world," I said.

She smiled. Nodded. Then tapped at a touch screen device that did the speaking for her now. "I also went waterskiing that day," the machine said.

"Wow," I said.

"That was last summer," she tapped into the machine.

Anne was 63 years old and, by that time, could not walk. ALS was shutting her down.

Amyotrophic lateral sclerosis — the dreaded "Lou Gehrig's disease" — is a neuromuscular disease that progressively paralyzes the body, robbing the person of all movement, including the ability to swallow and breathe.

Anne was trapped inside her failing body, fully aware.

When I wrote her obituary, I talked with Anne Schindler, who had been her editor at *Folio Weekly*.

"Her story makes you so aware of the things you take for granted, like the ability to take a breath," Schindler said.

I will never forget that line because it is so true.

She's gone now.

Time is short.

Take nothing for granted.

Live now, not later.

If you want to jump from that rock into a lake, then do it. Don't wait.

TAKE NOTHING FOR GRANTED

We wander through life, assuming it's always going to be there to live, and then crisis comes. I saw that with Anne, and with my mom, who suffered a paralyzing stroke at age 66. The message from their lives, and from their crises, is so important to many of the very successful and driven people I meet every day who miss the bigger picture in life.

I have a running joke with a woman I met who was a senior executive at a Fortune 5 company. We went to dinner the night I did a keynote for her organization. Her boyfriend called to tell her that the new couch had been delivered to the sitting area in their bedroom.

I saw her a couple of years later and asked her about the couch.

"You know, I've never even sat on it."

When I talked to her a couple of years after that, she still hadn't sat on that couch.

That's how her life is. It doesn't slow down long enough for her to sit on a nice couch, read a book, and drink in the moment.

I coach corporate people all the time on how to reconfigure their priorities. They know things are out of whack, but they feel so compelled to obsess about the professional challenge du jour that they have extreme difficulty extracting themselves from a lifestyle that isn't working for them on a soul level.

Why?

They feel like they have too much to lose. If they slow down and start living in a way that honors the priorities that truly matter to them, they may slow their career trajectory. They fear they will somehow fall behind or fall short or not have the cash they need to support the affluent lifestyle they currently enjoy. They won't be able to afford expensive couches that they don't have time to sit on. They won't have their opulent homes, showy cars, rich-lady jewelry, and extravagant one-week-a-year vacations.

I don't begrudge them any of the affluence that fills them with joy. But I have to wonder what they are missing out on because they are almost always working, thinking about working, or collapsing from working too much when they finally get to their lavish homes. They stress themselves out trying to be good to their families, trying to show up for the right events, trying to do everything they are "supposed" to do.

They can't seem to slow down long enough to even examine their lives and ask the hard questions.

Is it worth it?

Does it matter?

Do I actually love what I do?

Is there an easier way to do it?

I have seen the glassy-eyed look from corporate people who like what I say about life choices when I'm onstage but can't quite make that leap in their own lives. They want more fun, they want more fulfillment, and they're tired of living in a single dimension where they are defined by their work. They love their home life when they are in it, but they keep getting distracted by the never-satisfied beast of a J.O.B. that seduces them with money, power, and challenge.

So who is living the better life?

The person whose spectacular vacation costs $20,000 for a week?

The person who takes three weeks of vacation that cost a whole lot less?

Or the person who, like Anne, dares to dive into a few years of sailing around the world?

TRUE HAPPINESS

I do not judge people who make their work their priority. Not if their work makes them happy and secure. Not if they are truly happy.

My work is a priority for me. But it's not my only priority. It is no crime for me to say that my spirituality, family, and big picture of life matter more.

The problem is, I see a lot of people who are deluding themselves into thinking they're happy when, deep down, they aren't. They see their children growing up too fast — and without them. They aren't healthy. They're stressed by the life they lead and jealous of those who have found an easier way. They are usually the kinds of people I hear using the phrase, "Those of us who actually work for a living," as if those who don't work as hard as they do don't count.

I am not advocating that you quit your job.

I am not saying your work should not matter. It should.

I am not saying your life is meaningless if you don't reset your career demands to give you the elusive balance you keep hearing everybody talk about.

I am simply telling you that life is short, so you should make sure the path you are traveling is right for you. That you are learning and doing and growing in a way that makes the 24 hours you spend today the best 24 hours you could possibly spend.

If you are happy — truly happy — put this book down and go enjoy a beautiful day. If it ain't broke, don't fix it.

But if you're like most people in the "real" world, you probably have an inkling that there is more to life than the treadmill you are on. You may see others having better luck and more fun. Some of your friends may talk of deep spiritual or philosophical experiences, but you feel disconnected from their stories. You may be waiting for things to turn around.

At least you are noticing that there is more out there.

There are multitudes of people who live long lives without ever examining their choices or daring to deepen their experience. Life, good or bad, happens to them. They complain if things don't go their way but don't bother to find out what they can do to change things.

They wait. And then nothing changes.

People tell me about their train wreck of a marriage, a maniacal boss, their delinquent child. They tell me about their failures, their addictions, loved ones who have passed away, the weight they have gained.

They share good things, too, but they want help processing the bad things because those are the things that keep them stuck.

They know they are stuck.

They want things to be easier. They want to be happy.

Not just happy sometimes, but HAPPY overall.

"Make up your mind," I tell them. "You have to choose to be happy."

It's hard to hear. And it's even harder to change.

I did that. I made that choice. And when my life fell apart, I made that choice again, in the hardest possible way. Just because you choose happiness doesn't mean you will get it all the time because you will certainly face your share of unpleasant obstacles.

But, knowing you have made the choice to be happy means you will get to happiness, one way or another.

OPEN UP TO HAPPY

I can give all the tips and shortcuts in the world, but unless you make up your mind to live a meaningful, happy life, you aren't going to be happy. Unless you look inside of yourself and see someone who is worthy and wonderful, your subconscious won't accept that you deserve to be happy. Unless you open yourself up to it, it's not going to happen.

It is so simple to do, but so few people make that conscious choice. They feel happiness when it shines on them, but there are a lot of times when it isn't shining.

Is there some secret to making the sun shine?

Yes. It's not all that hard, once you open yourself up to it. And to those cynics who ridicule happy talk, I get the cynicism. As a former investigative reporter, I used to live with cynicism and negativity because most of what we did was point out what was wrong with the world and occasionally present a way to make it right. It was important work that helped to change the status quo, prompt new laws, and change lives, but everything was always viewed through a negative, critical, cynical filter.

Most people live in a world that is generally overcast. It is so part of the norm these days, and it's hard to escape. Believe me, before I chose to lead a happy life many years ago, I lived in an overcast world.

Eventually, I found that I really had the power to send the clouds away. I very seriously and deliberately made up my mind that I was going to be happy and poof! I was happy. In those times when the skies darken and bad things happen, that seed of optimism carries me through. Better days are coming.

You have the same right to be happy as anyone else.

From a spiritual perspective, you are just as important to this world as your boss, your CEO, and the president of the United States. God loves you every bit as much as anybody else and wants for you to be happy and fulfilled on your terms. It does not matter how wealthy, educated, successful, gregarious, connected, or popular you are. It doesn't matter what you look like or how beautifully you present yourself. You get the same chance at happiness as the next person.

But whether you achieve it or not is completely up to you.

There is an oft-plagiarized parable that was originally written by the late German author Heinrich Böll, who won the Nobel Prize for Literature in 1972. In his story, a tourist shows up in a European fishing village and sees a shabbily dressed fisherman asleep in his boat. He starts taking pictures of the man sleeping in this picturesque scene, and the sound of the camera shutter wakes the fisherman.

The tourist asks him why he isn't out fishing — the conditions are perfect for a big haul.

The fisherman says he'd already gone out for the day and caught four lobsters and a couple dozen mackerel. "I have enough for tomorrow and even the day after tomorrow," he says.

That's fantastic, the tourist says, but he implores the fisherman to imagine what he could catch if he went out a second, third, or even a fourth time. Then think of what might happen if he did that the next day and the next. By the end of the year, he would be able to buy himself a motor and another boat! In a few more years, he could afford a trawler. His company would catch so much fish, it could expand and have a store, a smoke house, a marinating factory. He could travel by helicopter, have restaurants, ship his fish straight to restaurants in Paris.

"What then?" the fisherman asks.

"Then you may relax here in the harbor with your mind set at ease, doze in the sunshine — and look out at the magnificent sea," the tourist says.

"But that is what I am doing right now," the fisherman says.

Ahhh.

So are you the tourist or the fisherman? And is that who you want to be? Make the choice.

IT'S YOUR LIFE

I'm definitely more fisherman. But that does not mean that I shirk my responsibilities to my career. I have always said that self-employment is a privilege that must be earned, and I earn it. But I consciously decide how much of my life I am going to give to my career, and I do have a very full life.

You are permitted to love the things you do outside of work more than your work. Just as you are permitted to love your work more than your outside life. You are allowed to think for yourself. It's your life.

Only yours.

If your boss wants more than you want to give, then you have to decide if you are going to give it — or go. If you don't make the sacrifice, you may be labeled as expendable.

No one owns you. And you own no one. At work, at home. You are the boss of you. You get one shot to live this life, so *live it.*

I was very moved by my interview with Brenda Barnes, who made *huge* headlines in 1997 when she left her job as CEO of PepsiCo North America to spend time with her family. Her children were 7, 8, and 10. It was so controversial — some decried her making that choice when she was such a visible role model. Yet she made the choice to live her own life, not somebody else's.

In 2004, she went back to work and was soon CEO of the Sara Lee Corporation, making her the most powerful woman in American business. In 2010, she was working out when she had a stroke. She had to leave her job.

Her daughter dropped out of school to take care of her.

I'm sure that Brenda never regretted that time out she took for her family. And then when she needed help, her family was there for her.

She knows how fragile and unpredictable life is. She knows there is no do-over.

She was interviewed at a Fortune conference and said, "Like a light switch, your life totally, totally changes. You can't do anything you used to do. You don't have the job you've had for 40 years and you are saying 'All I have to worry about is being able to walk.' Talk about changing priorities and milestones. You say, 'I hope someday I can walk.' You don't even begin to think about other things. It's, 'I've got to get back.'"

Her words force us to examine how we are living right now, to ask ourselves what we are taking for granted.

How is your life?

Is it *your* life?

You can do what you think is expected of you. You can chase what you think is most lucrative. You can hand over your entire schedule to other people who think they know what you should be doing with your time.

Or you can stop for a moment. Look at how you are spending your time. Ask yourself if, should some crisis occur, you will look back and wish you had lived these days differently?

If so, you have to wonder what's stopping you from taking charge of your life right now.

You are the one who decides what matters to you. Others may try to take charge of your time, but you decide your priorities. Only one person has the final say, and that is you.

Don't feel guilty because you have priorities that don't sync perfectly with the expectations of others. It is your life, not theirs.

I once had an editor who judged my passion for cycling, once sniping, "You love your bike more than your job." So what if I did? I loved my job, too! Interesting that she was still there at that newspaper the day it went out of business. I always wondered if she regretted giving most of her life, from her late 20s to her early 50s, to that company. Her world existed within the walls of that newsroom. Seriously, that was it. No love life. Very little recreation. An occasional vacation.

Then, with 24 hours' notice, that newspaper folded and went out of business. And she was unemployed.

Who was she without that job?

Who are *you* without *yours*?

Your loved ones.

Your things.

Your commitments.

Who.

Are.

You?

CHAPTER 3

THAT DESTINY THING

Every time I have veered off my intended path, it has been a mistake. A huge, miserable learning experience that I could have avoided if I'd just listened to that voice inside of me that said, "I. Don't. Want. This."

You cannot achieve balance if you are not true to your own personal path. You can make a situation functional, but not harmonious. Granted, there are times when you have to sacrifice harmony for function. If your spouse is diagnosed with cancer, you aren't going to walk off your miserable job and away from your insurance and paycheck until things settle down.

But know your path. Your destiny.

Soon after my first book was published, I was asked to be the senior editor of the alternative newspaper in Tampa. I was reluctant, but a close friend was going to be my boss, and she urged me to just try it. "If you don't like it," she said, "you can quit."

Hard Won Wisdom had just been on *Oprah* and was just starting to take off, but I didn't know how successful it would be or whether I was ever going to be able to turn "that speaker thing" into a viable career. What I knew was that I was being offered a weekly paycheck, health insurance, and the stability and financial security that had eluded me for nearly three years since I'd quit my job as a journalist to write my book.

It had been so long since I'd worked a job that the first day felt like it lasted for two months. I kept checking my watch. It's 2:07 p.m., 2:19 p.m., 2:23 p.m. — it was one of the longest days in my whole life, and things didn't get any better after that.

The politics of that company would wind up being the worst I'd ever seen, and there was a real saboteur in our midst. While my boss/friend was one of the best bosses I'd ever had, I was so miserable that I *looked* ill. I was hunched over. I couldn't sleep.

After seven insufferable weeks, a close friend called me at work and said, "I think you need to read *Hard Won Wisdom.*" She was joking about sending me to the self-help book I'd written, but I did exactly what she suggested and turned right to the page with my most important interview, with world-famous oceanographer Sylvia Earle, known as "Her Deepness." Earle's discussion of how we will never achieve our potential if we can't take risks was what motivated me to quit my journalism job in the first place.

I read the lines, "Many people resist risk and are only comfortable with the security of knowing, when they go to sleep at night, what the next day is going to be like. That's comforting. It's secure. And living like that is a choice they are free to make. ... Risk is a choice. It is the only way to test your potential."

After I read that quote, I walked into my friend's office and quit.

She was stunned.

All these years later, she'd be the first to say that what

happened was inevitable. I was destined to follow the path that led me to where I am, sitting here on a glorious Saturday, writing my eighth book and enjoying every single minute of it.

It's funny how, even though I have had these light bulb moments, I still get sidetracked. In the years since that decision, there were two times when I stepped off the path, and both times, it was a mistake.

I have learned to always listen to the voice that tells me where I should be walking. There is no tranquility or balance in my life when I am off course. I have occasionally taken a side trip off my path — usually to do something that seemed at the moment to be painless and lucrative — but it has been a mistake every time, either zapping my spirit or compromising my ability to take care of my own business.

HOW DO YOU FIND YOUR PATH?

Your path is already in you. Deep down inside. Ask yourself, what is your biggest dream? What is your passion? Who do you want to BE? It takes self-awareness to know your path, and a reset can help draw it out of you.

Once you figure out your path — which is really an ongoing journey of discovery — it takes real courage to keep walking. You will encounter distractions that pull you off course and obstacles that force you to defend your dream.

If you have been blessed with a dream, embrace it. Commit to it.

Imagine what Jeremy Fron faced, and the courage it took for him to leave Grand Rapids, Michigan and head to Alaska to be a fisherman. Everything fell apart the minute he got there. But he was called to live his fisherman dream, and doing that meant he had to fight for that privilege over and over again.

At age 20, he posted an online ad seeking work as a fisherman in Alaska. He got the call, paid his $800 airfare, and arrived on a frigid January day with less than $300 in his pocket.

The owner of the boat said he needed to put $1,000 worth of gas on Jeremy's credit card, but Jeremy started meeting people on the docks who told him that he was being scammed. He shouldn't be buying the gas, and he shouldn't have had to pay for his airfare, gear, or expenses.

He asked the boss what was going on, and the man kicked him off the boat.

Broke. Freezing. Alone.

"You can do the most when you are forced to do the most," he said. "When you are up against it — that is the moment you have to try your hardest. You don't have the option of giving up."

He found a very cheap room to rent and earned his keep by painting, shoveling snow, and chopping firewood.

"I am not college material. I knew I couldn't give up — I had to do it. That is where my courage came from. I used my towel as a towel, and my towel as a blanket. I was eating Ramen noodles."

Soon, he was fishing. The more he fished, the more he fished. His name got out there, and he was working every season — crab, long line, and salmon — throughout Southeast Alaska. He tells harrowing stories, like the boat starting to sink out in Dutch Harbor in the middle of January as 20-foot waves crashed into it. (The crew fought back and finally won with huge bilge pumps.) Then there was the time he fell overboard in 33-degree water when the air temperature was below zero. He was rescued just as his limbs stopped working. "Ten seconds longer and I'd have gone under."

He loves those stories because he is so passionately doing the work he loves.

He's done well. He owns two Florida homes, and he is only 26. He fishes the summer months in Alaska and flips houses in Florida the rest of the year.

"It is not a job," he said. "No fisherman does it for a job. It's a lifestyle. If we did it for a job, we'd hate it."

His story — and several others I will share here — show why you have to know your path and dare to honor it. Even when it is uncomfortable.

ONCE YOU FIND YOUR PATH

There will be hard choices you have to make about your path because passions can conflict. People may judge you for the choices you make, but you are the one who defines your path. They don't. Do what you must do.

It's your life. Live it in all of its dimensions.

Jeff Hipp was so consumed by his job that he had no idea what his wife had done to him behind his back.

Without asking him or mentioning it, she signed him up to coach T-ball for their 8-year-old daughter and 5-year-old son. She said nothing until it was time for him to go to the first meeting.

"I was angry," Jeff said. "I was working 10 or 11 hours a day and commuting on top of it. She told me, 'You are not spending enough time with your children.' I didn't know anything about being a coach, and I didn't like it. But I finally relented and, after a couple of months, I had more fun than any of the kids."

Soon he was coaching basketball and taking regular camping trips with the family.

Talk about a reset.

Next came another reset — at work — after he'd been promoted to branch manager in a very aggressive and intense specialty contracting company, where he oversaw the construction of schools, hospitals, semiconductor manufacturing facilities, and more. The money was great, and the job was prestigious, but it was crushing his soul.

"That's when a quart of vodka a night became a reality," he said. "It was no fun. It didn't matter what I did, what I tried. Everything I did was wrong with those people."

After two and a half years of that, he told his bosses he was quitting. They told him he couldn't, but they agreed to let him take a demotion back to senior project manager.

"Giving that up was one of the happiest days of my life," he said.

He stayed ahead of his debts, paid off his house, got the kids through school, then retired early.

Real early.

At 50.

It helped that he worked for an employee-owned company that he'd joined when it was on a massive growth swing. But it also helped that he wanted more life for himself, one where he skis every week in the winter, hangs with friends, works on his Oregon farm planting his olive grove, camps in the summer, and does "the childhood things I never could do when I was a kid."

He's the best retiree I've ever seen. Contrast that to some of his former colleagues who couldn't let go to retire.

"They get their self-esteem and self-worth out of their title," he said. "How can you create your image of who you are from just your position in a company? There is more to it than that. Your position in the company is a portion of your life. Not your entire life.

"My philosophy was, 'Know your exit point, and when you get there, exit.'"

When it seems like your life "is what it is," step back and ask yourself if it is what you *want*. Even when it functions well, it may not be functioning in a way that gives your soul the air it needs to breathe.

Kim Campbell was 27 years old, married to a wonderful man, and raising her stepson in northeastern Tennessee, close to her family and the life she'd always lived. She had a great job, too.

"But I was bored," she said.

She burned to go to law school, but how could she? She kept her dream to herself, secretly took the LSAT, then applied to Stetson University in Florida — more than 800 miles away.

No one in her family knew her plans, especially not her husband. She kept her mouth shut until the day she was accepted, when she told him she was moving to Florida to go to law school. He was not thrilled about it, but he stood by her.

She left her small-town existence to move to a metropolitan area with nearly three million people. All she brought with her from her old life were her two cats, Penelope and Muffin. But she knew she was on her path. When she got her law degree 2 ½ years later, she had also wrapped up her MBA.

Her husband, more than 20 years her senior, gave her an ultimatum. Come home or don't. Be married or get divorced.

She sought nothing in her divorce but freedom.

After making her mark as a lawyer, she ran for circuit court judge in Florida — no simple feat. She took the bench in 2013.

"I'm able to make people be better for themselves and their kids," she said. "If I had never made the decision to do this myself, I could not have preached it from the bench."

She remarried, has a little boy, and is someone so positively happy in her skin that it is hard to imagine her doing anything else.

Yet if she hadn't reset her life to travel the path she knew was her destiny, she'd still be in that small town, bored and unfulfilled.

I'm not saying you can't be fulfilled in a small town, or at a simple job, or that you shouldn't tell your family or spouse your dreams, or that they can't coincide. What I am saying is, be true to yourself.

When you follow your heart, there may be moments when you wonder if you're doing something wrong. You may see others "succeeding" wildly by doing the things you specifically chose not to do. Choosing to reset to a fulfilling life requires maturity and courage. You have to know you are right and be willing to let go of any "grass is always greener" thoughts that may spring up. Because you can't help but feel a few doubts every now and again.

The work-obsessed person feels a pang of jealousy because his friend has flexed his work schedule to give him enough spare time to surf every day.

And the surfer dude feels a pang of envy because his too-busy-to-surf friend just scored a huge win and is going to get a huge raise and promotion.

You decided how to live your life, and if you aren't "all in" with what you've created for yourself, either change what you're doing or change your attitude.

Dive into the life you choose without guilt or regret.

TREASURE EVERY MOMENT

The sunrise was spectacular as I walked the beach this morning. Calm water, cool sand — my own paradise. I said silently, "I am so lucky to be living this life."

I heard a voice inside of me answer, "No, you aren't. You *chose* this life. You *chose* to get up at 5 a.m. You *chose* to slow down to watch the sun come up and talk to the other people up so early on this beach. You *chose* it." Luck had nothing to do with it.

It made me feel pretty good about things because it's true. I did make those choices. It was Sunday, and almost everybody else was sleeping and missed the show. I got that special gift of the sunrise. But that does not mean the choice to sleep in would have been any less splendid — if it was a choice that I fully enjoyed.

Where we trip up is when we sleep in just because we went to bed when it was time to go to bed and woke up when we woke up, skipping the absolute pleasure of how great it feels to wake up rested and ready for the day. Or when we lose weeks doing our work without slowing down every day for a few minutes to say to ourselves, "Gee, I'm so lucky to be doing this," or "I really love doing this."

Do it consciously and with great, deliberate pleasure. Enjoy that exercise every single minute. Feel your heart beating and relish your strength. Breathe in your surroundings.

Your ordinary routine does not have to be dull. It can be mindful and fulfilling.

If you are going to live your destiny, *live* your destiny.

CHAPTER 4

GUT CHECK

Henry Hirsch was my favorite philosopher. He was also my uncle, and when I was in high school, he sat me down and told me this: "There will be times when you are going down the wrong path, and you will know it is the wrong path. Be strong enough to turn around."

He meant the advice for a young person facing peer pressure, but I carried that lesson into adulthood. It has kept me from doing the wrong thing in both my personal life and in business.

What a great reminder to listen to your gut, know what is right for you, and be bold enough to take action. It doesn't matter what others are pushing you to do or what others expect. What matters is the truth inside of you.

Always do a gut check.

What does that gut check tell you about your life? Are you doing something that you need to change? Does something feel wrong? Are you conforming to something that doesn't work inside of you?

Deciding to turn around and honor your truth is a reset moment, for sure.

It is so much harder to stand alone, true to yourself, than it is to do what everybody else is doing. But consider the following quotes:

Rita Mae Brown, the author, said "I think the reward for conformity is that everybody likes you except yourself."

And the poet E.E. Cummings said, "To be nobody but yourself in a world which is doing its best, night and day, to make you everybody else means to fight the hardest battle which any human being can fight; and never stop fighting."

We all conform, every single day. We know the rules of engagement out there. Some conformity isn't necessarily a bad thing.

I'd be more comfortable speaking onstage if I were performing in jeans, but I would never get hired, so I conform by suiting up. I don't use profanity onstage. I don't make political jokes. I respect the boundaries that ensure my success.

At home, I conform in the neighborhood. I make sure my house looks good and my grass is mowed — I like a nice house, but I also want the neighbors to be glad I am their neighbor.

If your paycheck depends on it, you likely have no choice but to try to blend into a work culture or other environment that has rules you don't like. But you don't have to stay forever. And when you are on the wrong path, you need a strategy to turn around.

There is a huge difference between choosing to honor the rules and completely selling out. There is conformity that is a bad thing. And understanding the difference is a lifelong learning process. You figure out what you can live with and what you can't. We all have times when we have to mute — or just tone down — our true self. But muting doesn't mean trampling.

The ultimate question is this: Is it worth it to conform? If you feel like it is compromising your authentic self, it is time to check in with your gut. If you aren't being true to yourself, it may be time for a reset.

It's a whole lot easier to live in your skin if you make conscious decisions about how you are going to conform. Balance is key. You *can* conform without selling out.

Aren't there times when conformity is comforting? Aren't there times when it is easier to be welcomed into the fold when you know what you need to do? Do you like being in the "in group," the "out group," or no group at all?

Conformity becomes a problem when, in order to blend in, you are required to do it — and you don't want to. There comes a point when you have to ask whether being accepted is worth sacrificing pieces of your true self. If that sacrifice is too painful, it's time to start thinking about an exit plan.

When you are exhausted by the pressure to look and act and be like people that you don't want to be like, you need to decide what you are going to do. It's time to find an environment where you are celebrated and not minimized.

TRADING CONFORMITY FOR ...

I recently had dinner with a corporate executive who takes home more than $1.5 million a year in pay and options.

That amount of money is staggering.

Can you imagine it? Year after year?

It's raining money all over him, yet he is *miserable*. He hates the psycho-politics in his company. His family never sees him. He had a heart attack — at age 49! He now has to politick his way into a good position while the company restructures again, and he always has to kiss up to people he neither likes nor respects.

"I can't stand it," he said. "I hate myself when I'm at work. I'm ashamed of some of the things I've done there. But I can't let go. I have too much at stake."

Exactly what is at stake?

Is it worth it?

How can it be?

On the outside, this guy is the model of success. But he's traded his soul for it. And isn't that the worst kind of failure?

He even had a gut check and admitted he couldn't stand it, but he did nothing about it. How sad to live in such unhappiness. And for what?

In this life, our challenge is to find our path and deepen our souls by traveling that path with integrity and courage. Are you on the right path? You are allowed to ask that question — in fact, you *must* ask it. And if your conclusion is that you are not living your truth, make some changes. Reset.

We were warned about succumbing to peer pressure when we were kids, and we either held strong or caved. But what about that same pressure as we grow older? What happens when we wake up one day and realize we are conforming to a norm that violates our own personal truth? What happens when our job or our friends or our lifestyle clashes with our conscience?

Does it feel like you have veered off course? That the life you are living isn't honoring your values or goals? Do a gut check.

There will be times when you are going down the wrong path and you will know it is the wrong path. Be strong enough to turn around.

Just like Uncle Hank said.

CHAPTER 5

THE "AS SOON AS …" TRAP

As soon as you lose 15 pounds …

As soon as you finish your degree …

As soon as you can afford to …

As soon as the kids are old enough to be left alone …

As soon as you retire …

What if "as soon as" never comes? Why sacrifice a day or a week or a month or a year trying to get through one ordeal and the next and the one after that, delaying happiness until things settle down? Life is chaotic. There will always be some new lesson thrown at you that will grow you — but also distract you. There is always a challenge.

I was showing my doctor pictures from a weekend kayaking trip. She looked wistfully off into space and said, "One day, when I have a life again …"

"Seriously?" I asked her. "You have to wait to have a life?"

"I have a life," she said. "My kids and my patients."

That *is* a lot of life.

But if she doesn't keep a sliver of life just for herself, she'll lose her identity to her obligations. If she doesn't live life *now*, then she may never get the chance.

What do you wish you could do in life? And what are you waiting for?

A lot of people postpone living until things are just right. As if there will be a moment when everything is in order.

Things are never "just right" for long. Everything will be in order for a few hours or maybe a day, and then something will happen that will remind you that the only real order in life is disorder.

When you have a problem, you have a natural desire to know that everything will work out fine. You crave the certainty and comfort of resolution. When you get it, you relax. But guess what? It won't be long before another problem presents itself. That is how life unfolds. Who gets a stress-free ride with no adversity?

It would be nice. But it would also be pretty boring.

There was a time when everything was perfect in my life. It was a *very* short time — just one night in 1990 when I was in my 20s. I slept so well that night! But life intruded the next morning, and I learned something important: You have a lot less stress when you stop stressing about this thing or that thing that could be better.

IT'S A TRAP

How many people think they could solve everything if they could just hit the Powerball? No money worries, just an endless party, right? But there are so many news reports chronicling the lives of jackpot winners whose worlds became hell after winning.

How many people aspire to be actors? Yet there are so many movie stars who are chronically unhappy, despite the fact that they are rich, thin, beautiful, and revered. There are a million gazillionaires who are lonely, unhealthy, or lost.

Having money or having every*thing* you ever wanted does not fix what is already wrong within you. If you can't be happy with your current set of problems, you probably won't be happy with the next set of problems, either – unless you make a mental shift and decide it is time to be happy.

Years ago, I was the writing coach to a multimillionaire who wanted to be an author. On the outside, he seemed to have it all. He had multiple mansions, his own marina, and a golf course. He was a generous man, yet he was a terrible alcoholic who could also be quite abusive.

One day, we attended a conference then worked on his manuscript at a hotel in St. Louis. The housekeeper came in, and he handed her a $20 bill and told her he would not be needing the room cleaned.

She smiled broadly and clutched it to her chest.

"I give all of these tips to my church," she said, beaming. There was such light emanating from her!

I looked at her, then looked at him. Most people would think he had everything and she had nothing, but that was wrong. She had it all, and *he* had nothing. Her life was full and meaningful. He was angry and lost. A few years later, he fell down the stairs and lost his mobility. His money ran out. His family was a mess. It didn't matter whether he was rich or poor. He remained the unhappiest person I have ever known.

Isn't it sad that the reward you expect to enjoy when things fall into place does not give you the liberation that you could give yourself right now?

WE ARE ALL FRAGILE

I have often talked about Kristine Fugal Hughes, who founded Nature's Sunshine Products with $150 and an idea. She had no college degree and seven children, and she turned that vitamin business into a company that turns well over $400 million in profit each year.

"That's amazing," I told her when I interviewed her. "What's your leadership style?"

"What you see is what you get," she started. "I got my hair cut in high school into a pixie cut. It's always been that way. I don't even put on enough pretense to curl my hair. I put on my mascara, put on my lipstick, then put on the clothes that fit me because I'm overweight, and I just go out into the world and do my best."

"Stop," I said. "Let's talk about your weight."

Her sigh was audible, and her voice cracked.

"Do you know how hard it is to stand in front of a vitamin company and be fat?" she asked.

I'd just read a magazine article on her. She had multiple homes. Tons of money. A big family. A life that almost everyone in the world would envy.

And yet she was as fragile on the inside as most of the rest of us. This was my most life-changing moment in all of the interviews I have done for all of my books. Because of what she said, I asked all of the leaders I interviewed for my first book whether they had self-esteem issues.

Only five said they did not. I have long joked that I believe four of the five were lying.

That revelation taught me so much. Happiness, self-awareness, and self-esteem are not the reward for hard work and success. They are right there in front of us if we dare to seek them for our lives *right now.*

Liberation, validation, and reward do not come to us "as soon as" we get to where we are trying to go. You can enjoy those things today. Even if you have a lot of room for improvement, they're there for you.

Today.

Right now.

Not "as soon as" you get past this current set of obstacles. Not once you look the way you think you should look or have the job you think you should have or move into the house that you think is perfect for you. Happiness can begin this minute.

Just make the decision.

Be. Happy. Now.

Be. Secure. Now.

Be. Alive. Now.

Reset.

STATE OF WANT

As humans, we cause ourselves a lot of grief by our insatiable "state of want."

We want more.

We want different.

We want it now.

A state of want belittles the present. Things would be great, if only ...

Well, things *are* great. If you are not starving or suffering or in real fear, you've got a lot. One-fourth of the world's population has no electricity, more than a billion people don't have clean drinking water, and nearly half of the world's population lives in poverty on less than $2.50 a day.

And you don't let yourself feel happy because you are feeling chunky? Or because you haven't gotten as high up the ladder as you want to go? Or because you haven't found the right person to "complete you"?

Complete yourself, because you are very, very rich.

Stop focusing on lack and refocus your attention on what you already have. You are already blessed!

Happiness comes when you stop focusing on what is missing and start focusing on the abundance that already surrounds you. If you aren't hungry, in pain, or scared, you are living a life that millions of people around the world would do anything to experience.

So enjoy it. Don't delay your love of life. Reset. Choose to love it right now.

I live near the best beaches in the country, and I go all the time. But I have legions of friends who will not go with me because they don't want to be seen in their bathing suits. They deprive themselves of the glory of our home state of Florida because they don't want anyone to see their cellulite.

Do they actually think it is going to get all that much better? Weight goes up, it goes down. There is always room for improvement. I have only two friends who have phenomenal bathing beauty bodies. Does that mean the rest of us should put on muumuus and hide in caves? And does anyone else care about our weight as much as we do, anyway?

I have always had a weight issue — and there was a time when I weighed a *lot* more than I do now. But there was never a time when I would deprive myself of my joy of the beach. So what if I wasn't a *Sports Illustrated* model? And so what if someone stared at my fat butt or big thighs?

Of course I wanted to be thinner. But I was unwilling to delay one minute of my life because of it.

Are you delaying yours?

Why?

You're not getting younger.

Time is always running out.

Why deprive yourself of adventure, love, and meaning in your life? Why have an enormous bucket list on hold for the day when you will finally be able to do what you really want to do? Why wait until things are "just right" to let go and relax?

You can do so much living by freeing yourself from your normal duties — even if just for a weekend. Stop waiting to live. Take your life off hold. Go with what you've got. There are so few moments when everything is in place, so stop hesitating and start living. You can do it now!

Life gets hard, then it gets easier. Then it gets hard, then it gets easier all over again. Roll with it.

TRUE SUCCESS

Real success is an inner quest. It's something you define for yourself when you get up each morning, and you either achieve it or don't achieve it by the end of the day. The only thing you can really have is this moment — this day. You can achieve huge emotional success on any day, and every day.

Or you can live by default.

Your success in this day has nothing to do with a to-do list. What matters is how you are *living* this day.

Most people define their day by having to be in a certain place at a certain time to do a certain thing to achieve a certain outcome.

Instead of measuring your days by how much you get done, measure them by how well you have lived and how deep you have gone. If you define your day with challenge, hope, people, passion, maturity, growth, learning, development, spirituality, and other such things, you can achieve meaningful success every day. You'll be happier with a personal checklist like that.

It may not make others happy because there are many people who want to hand you a set of priorities, but *you* get to decide why you are here. You — and only you — define your purpose.

You are in control. You don't have to "give" this day to anyone or anything. You aren't required to relinquish the present to anyone so they can give you some sort of prize later on, like a paycheck or a promotion. Yes, you have to show up for work and do a good job. Yes, you have other obligations in life. You have to pay bills and tend to daily living. But you have a choice in how you do those things.

You are allowed to keep your own emotional space. You can tend to your many obligations. But don't hand over your emotional growth just because you have so many demands on your time and energy. Your life, your soul, your day is yours.

What are you waiting for? Reset.

You can't always do what you want to do, when you want to do it, because the demands of the day can make some things impossible. If you are an accountant in tax season, you can't spontaneously jump in the car to hike the Appalachian Trail for a week. You might not even be able to run out to Chili's for dinner. But you can center yourself. Feel good about what you have. Send a couple of e-mails thanking people for being in your life. Slow down enough to enjoy your dinner. Go online and make a charitable contribution. Just because you are in a high-stress moment doesn't mean you have to pass on seizing the day and defining it with purpose.

When we were kids, my brother and I used to shout, "Dessert first!" That's the way to live. Why wait?

Take nothing for granted. The tomorrow you expect may not be the tomorrow you get. No doubt, you've heard many times about someone who worked and worked and saved and saved, planning for the dream retirement. Then retirement came, and so did the cancer diagnosis. Or the stroke.

You can't ignore the future, and you *should* plan for it. By all means, have a good plan for your life. A plan gives you direction. But be aware that it may be the best piece of fiction you will ever write. Self-confidence is what will keep you moving forward when the plan falls apart.

Live in that "sweet spot" that is somewhere between planning for nothing and planning for everything. You don't want to spend every dime and wind up retiring with nothing to show for all of your years of effort. Nor do you want to retire with all the money in the world but without the health to enjoy it.

FIND YOUR PURPOSE

Back when I was struggling so hard to become a published author, I joined a women's group that would meet and process our lives. At one gathering, we bandied about our ideas for the topic du jour when I blurted, "I don't know what my purpose is."

I had quit my job to write that book, yet I could not

find a publisher. If I was not going to be Fawn Germer, the author, *who* was I going to be?

"I don't know mine, either," said my friend Teresa.

"Me, either," said Pam.

"I don't know," said Tami.

One by one, every one of us admitted we did not know our purpose in life. As we went around the room, I felt certain that Bette Haase would be able to enlighten us, seeing as how she had ovarian cancer and was taking chemo. Certainly that experience had shown her the meaning of life.

But when her turn came, Bette shrugged.

Over the next year, we all walked our paths. I persevered and found a publisher. Teresa went back to school to become a nurse practitioner. Tami went back to school to become a nurse anesthetist. Pam got a new job.

And Bette? She kept living. She hiked, she traveled, she laughed.

She was there for my first book signing, a gift of presence that I know drained her. I visited her in the hospital the day before leaving on my book tour. It was the first time she acknowledged she knew she was dying.

When I finished my tour, Bette was starting her decline. I was so impressed by how her family had closed ranks around her. Each of her seven siblings took a weeklong shift in her caregiving. Her son was by her side the whole time.

I wrote her obituary. And when I wrote it, I thought back to the day when we were all stumped about our purpose in life. Throughout her illness, Bette dove into her life.

I remember going kayaking with her to Caladesi

Island State Park on a beautiful December day. She dove into that frigid water.

"Are you *crazy*?" I shouted. No Floridian in her right mind would ever do that, but she did.

"It's beautiful!" she shouted back.

The way she lived — really lived — taught me the simple answer to our purpose in life.

Your purpose in life is to *live* your life.

I wrote about that in her obituary and then, running late, headed out into the night to get my hair cut and colored before heading to St. Louis for a speech the next morning.

I was very late for my appointment and had never been to that salon before so I didn't know exactly where it was. I couldn't see the addresses and tried driving in the turn lane to get a better look. It was a huge mistake, one that almost cost me my life because I was about to smash head-on into another car.

With one split second left, the other car found a hole in the traffic, exited the turn lane, and missed me.

My heart was pounding. My friend had died after spending two years fighting to live every day. And I had almost thrown my life away by not paying attention. It was a lesson I have never forgotten.

We waste so much life by not paying attention. We get lost in our work and the drama and our devices, and we forget that living — real living — requires conscious action. Attention.

The only time you know you have for sure is right now. So live *now*, not as soon as ...

CHAPTER 6

BALANCING IT OUT AT WORK

I will often ask my audience members to raise their hands if they check their work e-mail after they go home at night. At least three-fourths of the hands go up. Just as many say they do it at least twice. At least half say they do it three or more times.

Because of technology, it is possible to work 24 hours a day — and still not be done.

Why do we do this?

It's hard to pull away from something that does not stop pulling at you, and the world is filled with jobs that will not quit pulling. I just moderated a panel and asked my panelists if the number of hours they work has changed much over the years. One woman said she's kept the same hours throughout her career: from 8 a.m. to 7 p.m., then from 10 p.m. to 2 a.m. Every day. That's 15 hours a day. She loves her work.

If you love your work and your hours, keep doing what you are doing. No need to reset.

But if it feels like you are missing something by working too hard or too long, a reset may well be in order.

HOW DO YOU DEFINE SUCCESS?

What is success? Kathy Casey sure had it. She had an extremely high-profile job as Vice President/General Manager at the Kellogg Company, responsible for a $2 billion budget and a team of hundreds. She traveled more than 100,000 miles a year. She was visible and racing on the fast track.

But something wasn't right.

"Unconsciously, I'd started making choices to put my career first," she said. "I missed my Grandma's funeral for a meeting and worked to the point that it impacted my health and my relationships with those that I love. I was focused on chasing the next job, the next title, the next challenge. It's an addiction."

She missed her son's first birthday, celebrating it instead on a different day. She told herself it didn't really matter. He was a baby and he wouldn't know the difference. But she did.

"I started to not like who I saw in the mirror," she said.

She'd always been poised for that kind of success. Her mother used to joke that Kathy, the middle child, started working on her resume when she was six. She started counting the lunch money in kindergarten, winning the spelling bee, getting involved in student government, and being editor-in-chief of the school paper.

That kind of Type A mindset made her a natural for the executive ranks, but once she was in them, something was very wrong. The sense that there was so much more to life than what she was experiencing led her to do something drastic.

"At some point, I recognized I was starting to resent other peoples' lives. I was envious of people who had time for themselves and their families. I wanted more freedom and flexibility."

She reset.

She said no to two promotions that required extensive commuting or relocation. She requested a less demanding assignment that reduced her stress and gave her more time at home.

She is still a VP of Sales for Kellogg, but her job does not carry nearly the same responsibility or stature.

"Now my role is smaller in scope. It was a decision that said I no longer wanted a bigger job."

She took herself off the fast track.

"I stopped chasing the rainbow with the missing pot of gold," she said. "What is interesting is that, with a redefined set of life boundaries, I am doing some of my best work yet."

And she likes who she is.

"What matters to me now is that I am there when people need me," she said.

When my mom and dad died, Kathy made an effort to call me. Every single day.

"I am significantly happier and I am more present in my daily life," she told me. "I have more energy to give back. I think that a lot of people think, 'One more job, one more raise, one more level — then I'll get there. Then I'll be happy.' But you are working more and having more stress and your life isn't any richer because of it."

The choices you make about how you spend your time and energy are choices with real consequences.

"If it feels bad, you probably made the wrong decision. Redefine success," she said.

IS IT WORTH IT?

I reset my life balance long ago when I was a 24-year-old reporter in Jacksonville, Florida. I'd worked more than 80 hours that week, and our bosses were especially prickly about uncompensated overtime because they had just lost a wage and hour lawsuit. My boss sent me into administrative assistant Joyce Duarte's office to revise my time card.

Joyce just stared at it.

"Gee, Fawn, is it really worth it?" she asked.

I froze in place because, even though she said nothing else, I knew exactly what she was saying. Money is nice, but time is irreplaceable. Work is important, but it is not everything.

That same week, a friend did a late-night stopover to the newsroom to pick up something she'd forgotten.

"Why am I still here?" I asked her.

"Because your life is meaningless, and this is all you have," she teased.

We both laughed. But her words, timed so soon after what Joyce had said, marked a turning point for me. From then on, I treated my time like it was priceless — because it was.

It was the beginning of a lifelong reset that rescued me from being what is classified as an "insecure overachiever" and turned me into a happy human being. I have always had a fulfilling personal life, even when it came at the expense of my professional life.

The choice really didn't hurt me. I'm sure I could have done more, but I've done enough. My goal was to suck every bit of life out of every single day — and I've done that.

How about you?

The thing that baffled me most when I went into management as a newspaper editor was how many of my reporters waited until deadline to even *start* writing their stories. As a reporter, I never missed deadline. Ever. It was a mark of diligence and reliability, but I also had another motivation.

I wanted to go home.

My work was my work, but it was not my life.

Once I became an editor, I couldn't leave until everything was edited and "in the can." I would cajole, wheedle, push, bribe, or sternly remind my reporters that deadline performance was mandatory, but it didn't seem to matter. Those who were chronically late in the beginning were still chronically late in the end.

Why would some people choose to linger at work when they could have been home with their families, enjoying a social event, working out, or playing outdoors? Why would certain people wander in on the weekend for no apparent reason — especially when it was a beautiful day outside?

Interestingly, the people who kept hanging around weren't my best performers.

Do you work to live or live to work?

I know, that's a tired old question.

But it really is *the* question, and it's worth asking and re-asking at different stages in your life. It doesn't matter which way you answer it, as long as the answer meshes with your goals and dreams.

It is pretty common for people to think that their way is the best way. That you should react and respond as they would. That what motivates them should motivate *you.* So if you are more motivated to work than your colleagues, don't judge them, because you don't want them to judge you, either. Your right to work a 60-hour week is only as valid as the next person's right to work 40.

I don't want to show you how to reset your life so yours can be just like mine. You don't need to be living my life — I do. I don't need to be living your life — you do.

You don't need to be living according to anyone else's definition of purpose and fulfillment. The only thing that matters is what *you* think and how you set your boundaries to honor what matters to you.

So I've just got to ask you: Is your life showing any signs of balance? Here are a few questions. Just circle the number in either column as you agree or disagree with each statement:

	Agree	Disagree
Do you love your work?	0	1
Does it give your life as much as it takes?	0	1
Do you feel out of control when it comes to your time?	1	0
Do you have alone time to do something for yourself at least twice a week?	0	1
Do you use all of your vacation time?	0	1
Do you feel overwhelmed?	1	0
Do you feel guilty leaving work for personal obligations?	1	0
Do you feel guilty at home because you don't have enough time to be the kind of parent, spouse, or family member you want?	1	0
Do you feel you have enough time for your family and loved ones?	0	1

	Agree	Disagree
Are you spending time working after you get home?	1	0
Do you feel stressed much of the time?	1	0
Do you make time for fun every week?	0	1
Are you always rushing from one thing to the next?	1	0
Are you consciously living in the moment?	0	1
Are you happy most of the time?	0	1
Do you feel like other people have more control over your time than you do?	1	0
Do you resent people who do have more time to live a balanced life?	1	0
Is your life overscheduled?	1	0
Do you usually feel caught up with things?	0	1
Do you think you will regret how you are spending your time?	1	0
Total Points		

Scoring:

Add up the points in each column.

If you have 7 or more points: Consider this your wake-up call. Your life balance is out of whack. You may like it that way, but if you don't, you need to make changes to give you more control over your time. Reset!

4-6 points: You are out of balance, but it looks like you are consciously taking steps to control things. Decide whether your way of life is working for you, and if it is, bravo. If it isn't, reset.

0-3 points: Skip this chapter. Your balance is in check in a crazy-making world.

There are always times in life when we are way out of balance. Just ask an air conditioner repairman in the middle of August or the parent of a newborn. That's how it goes. But over time, if you realize you are living in a single dimension and that is not enough, look inside yourself. Are you deliberately making choices about how you are spending your life? Have you set the necessary boundaries that can give you more control? Are you living by design or by default?

Sometimes, you get a message like Pete Foley did.

Pete always worked hard because he a) loved his work and b) had a wife and four children.

"I've been in the habit of working whenever and however long it takes to get done what must be done," he said. All of his careers — whether writing or coordinating large events — were demanding and stressful.

In 2008, he was diagnosed with Stage IV esophageal cancer — "a radical, eye-opening experience." Now that is behind him, he has a dramatically different perspective on life.

"I know I danced with death," he said. "… When I revisit the experience, it's a healthy reminder to remember that work should be rewarding, love should permeate every dimension of your life, and you really should do stupid things like jump smack-dab in the middle of a mud puddle when you have your 'Sunday best' on. You only live once, right?"

Live the life that matters.

THE SOURCE OF YOUR WORK DRIVE

I wanted a lot of outside input for this chapter because I have clearly chosen the "big picture" version of my life over any career obsessions. What is it that drives people to work so hard?

Some people, like Kim Feil, just love working. Kim is one of my most successful friends — and definitely one of the least pretentious. She's been the chief marketing officer for Office Max, Walgreens, and Sara Lee. When Office Max merged with Office Depot and moved its headquarters to Florida, she decided to stay put. No leaving Chicago for her.

She definitely does not need the paycheck, yet she chooses to keep at it. Between gigs, we hung out at the beach as she debated two job opportunities that would be her next re-invention. One was to be the CEO of a promising startup. The other was to run the largest association and stand at the forefront of the retail industry.

Great jobs. But why work so hard when she doesn't have to? What is it that drives her?

"Only rarely in my career have I 'worked.' I gain energy from my passion for learning new things, building new things, meeting new people, and tackling challenges with outcomes that are rewarding. If that's called work, then okay."

She ended up taking the job as CEO of bizHive, a "marketing marketplace" to match small businesses with marketing products.

"Now, I'm embarking on another path to be CEO of a startup venture and grow as an entrepreneur for the next 30 years," she said.

If you do the math, it means she'll be working well into her 80s. But that's what drives her.

I'll be kayaking. That's what drives me.

Each calling is perfectly valid — just different.

I asked my friend Maureen McGurl why she continues to work so hard when she could simply retire and live the good life.

"Because I love being in the game," she said. It was as if I was talking to someone just starting her career. Her love of her work is in her being. Work is as exciting for her as kayaking is for me. Maybe more. So she should work. It makes her happy. It fulfills her.

And if your work is making you that happy, keep doing it!

Are you happy working like you are working? Because your relationship with work is a choice. Most of us have to do something in order to pay the bills. But just how deep we dive in is something we control, with choices about how much we want to work or how much we spend (requiring us to get the right-sized paycheck).

Don't buy into the whole martyr hierarchy, where the person who works twice as many hours is twice as important. Not true. What does it mean to humanity when one person spends 60 hours scouring purchase orders and another spends only 40? Is the 60-hour person more critical to the fabric of humanity? No.

You can't assume the person who works fewer hours than you is a slacker any more than that person can assume you're out of balance and one-dimensional. And vice versa.

For some, work is what provides inner balance.

My father worked as a pharmacist until he was 84. He already had what he wanted and needed, but I know that the final years of his career kept him alive because his work gave his life purpose. He didn't want to retire.

"The best thing about my job is that I work hard, eight hours a day, five days a week. But when I leave work, I leave it there. I never worry or even think about my job when I am not working. That is priceless."

— *Michael Ryan, airport customer service agent, Delta Airlines*

"I work about 50 hours, so 10 hours are unpaid. I do it so I won't be tortured by things undone during my free time."

— *Patti Ivey, project administrator with the Florida Department of Transportation*

"I work between 45 and 60 hours a week. I'm in the analytic consulting business, helping banks combat money laundering and terrorist financing. Our work week depends on our projects and the need to travel. I took this job because I can work primarily at home and can maintain 50 percent custody of my 7-year-old daughter. I am regularly offered jobs that pay considerably more, but they would require me to move away from my child – which I am unwilling to do."

— *Jim West, anti-money laundering statistician*

"After having our third child, I resigned my full-time job to do part-time contract work, 20 to 30 hours a week. With three children, ages 7, 4, and 1, that's all I can give and make sure I can meet the needs of my family. It means my career takes a pause, but if I were working full time, I am certain I would fail both my family and my employer."

— *Robin Semadeni, sales and marketing consultant for Frito-Lay*

"We are required to work 45 hours, but I am typically between 50 and 55. It takes that many hours to stay on top of my business. We have so many meetings that I have to get my real work done at some point."

— *Kim Tisdale, manager of accounts payable, Walmart Inc.*

I work 40 hours, as required, and not a minute more! It just isn't worth it to do more. The job won't love you back, and when it comes time to make cuts, it's the people that everyone wants to drink with that get to keep their jobs."

— *Merrilee Stanley, architect*

Unfortunately, workplace cultures can eliminate the option for choice. Some don't care about your need for balance. It is very, very common for some companies to demand backbreaking, all-or-nothing commitment. If you want to work in those companies, you have no choice but to play by their rules. Your only choices are whether to sign up and stay, or go.

"Climbing the ladder and gaining financial security meant everything to me," said Patricia Simmers, a single parent and senior financial officer in the Denver area. "I have often worked many extra tireless hours throughout my career."

I am interested in the work people choose to do. But I am *fascinated* by *why* they do it with varying degrees of intensity. What would make someone work 50, 60, 70, 80 or more hours every week? For them, work is life, and everything else must be squeezed in. Maybe there is time for a quick workout — at 4 a.m. And time to squeeze in an hour of quality time with the family. Life fills the tiny little cracks in a schedule that is work, work, work.

Why work so hard? Erin Himelhoch, 32, put it in the simplest terms: "I'm motivated by money. I'm very independent, and it's important that I take care of myself." Erin is my cousin's daughter and one of my favorite thirty-something people on earth. But we sure are different.

"What do you think of people who say, 'Need less, spend less, work less, live more'?" I asked her.

"I think they're hippies," she answered flatly.

Cracked me up.

When she started her career, she worked 12- to 14-hour days. She's scaled it back some to have a little bit of a social life, she told me, but she has only dialed it back to a 55-hour workweek.

Not a lot of improvement, but she's a senior mortgage banker who has done very well for herself.

Why do you work like that? I asked her.

"Because I am materialistic," she said. "I'm already working fewer hours than I used to. I have a lot of hobbies already. I don't know what I would do with much more free time."

I didn't think it was only materialism. I asked her what makes her happy.

"Being able to take care of myself, help my friends and family, travel, have a nice house, car, purse ..." she said. "The work I do gives me a sense of fulfillment — like I've made good use of my time. Every loan I write changes a person or a family's life. I have also been saving for retirement, so my mantra is, 'More hard work now so I can play later.' I want to retire early and live well."

People are different. As long as Erin is happy, that's all that matters.

Contrast her with Lisa Kruckeberg, 34, who had an awakening in 2012 when she lost six loved ones, got divorced, and left her job of 10 years.

"It was excruciating just to survive," she said. "But I still had a spark, and that spark has grown into a raging fire. My life is like a phoenix. It was broken, a pile of ash on the floor, but from that has grown a world of gratitude, forgiveness, understanding, and joy. Life is good, if we just get out of our own way and let it be."

She completely reset into a larger-than-life character who could be a guru for me.

"We only get so many trips around the sun," she said. "I don't want to waste any of them. I think one of the best things any of us can do for ourselves is decide what is important to us, not what society thinks is important or what we have to project. For me, that is family, friends, fitness, fun, and function. Every day, I think about those five things and make choices to put those things at the top of my list."

What she said is really worth noting because she was able to rattle off her priorities so quickly. She knows what she wants. She has taken the time to do the inner self-examination that will deliver her fulfillment.

What are your priorities?

The last we connected, Lisa was training to climb Mt. Rainier, doing volunteer work, and spending time with family and friends. "I wake up with a smile on my face, and I go to bed with peace in my heart," she said.

Finally, think of how she is living and then add this to it: Lisa was just promoted to be a regional vice president for the Principal Financial Group. She has some 55-hour workweeks, and some where she doesn't crack 40. But she is definitely on the fast track *and* living the life she wants to live.

The only way to "have it all" is to have it all on the inside so you are free to make decisions that matter to you, not others. If you do not have to impress others, satisfy expectations, or achieve some sort of "potential," you are free to look inside of yourself and focus on doing what *you* want to do.

Do you know anyone who is doing a job because he or she needs to do something, and it provides a paycheck and benefits? Of course you do. Is that you? I sure hope not. I hope you have work that stirs your passions.

Linda Hilliard-Bogan used to be in sales, but she wound up working with autistic children after her niece was diagnosed with autism. After that, she kept doing human services work as she helped children with anger issues, then people with drug and alcohol issues.

"I work about 50 hours a week, and I emotionally take the job home," she said. "I even sneak files home to work on them, as well. I'd do it even if I didn't have to work — but I'd do it my way."

You can feel her passion for what she is doing, and the sacrifice she makes is not a sacrifice to her.

If you are going to spend 40 or more hours a week doing something, it should be something that you love, because when you love it, it's not really work.

Patrick Burgess doesn't stop working. That's because he uses his engineering background with his creative brain to invent new products. I've seen him design everything from medical equipment to office chairs to recreational gear.

"I love what I do, so I could argue it's not really work," he said. "I also never really stop working, even when I'm changing a diaper, because I'm thinking about better ways to make a diaper bag."

There is a huge difference between someone who is passionate about work and someone who is a workaholic. A workaholic can't take a time-out because that break makes them uncomfortable. Off duty, they compulsively check their phones for e-mails, texts, or other work prompts. They pride themselves on working through their illnesses and never taking vacations. Control is so important to them that they can't let go or delegate to others because they are certain that anyone else will screw things up. They do all of this at the expense of living. Family is supposedly important, but when it comes to choosing a baseball game or recital over more work, they choose work. Or they take work with them so they can be present physically, but they're definitely not there emotionally.

"I work 60 hours, minimum, and have been doing so for 30 years. Yeah, I bitch and moan at times, but if I didn't like doing it, I figure I'd stop. And when the magazine comes out each month, I look at it and don't regret the hours."

— *David Claude Bailey, Senior Editor,*
O. Henry Magazine.

"I work way more than everyone around me — 50 to 60 hours a week. I do it because, as a single mom, the job is critically important to us. Plus, I have always had an internal drive to deliver results. It's in my DNA. The good news is that I can balance it all. I have not missed any of my daughter's soccer games, school plays, and activities, or horse shows. It's in the wiring."

— Liz Corey, Director of Global Talent Acquisition, Masonite

"I've cut back to 35 hours. I work less than others around me. I love working less so I can do other things, but it's also hard because I have to fight against feeling like a slacker. I think society expects more of me, even though in my younger years I did work many, many, more hours."

— Kathy Trousdale Lee, professional nanny

"I now work 40 hours or less a week, but there have been times when I worked 70 to 80. In fact, I once worked seven weeks without a day off … Hard work has given me more or better things, but I'm not sure it has given me a better life."

— Bruce Heaton, General Manager, Hogs and Heifers Saloon of Las Vegas

A Wayne State University study on the personality traits of workaholics found that a lot of workaholics have an unrealistic sense of self-importance regarding who they are and what they are accomplishing. They believe that, without their contribution, everything will fall apart at work. They also have an unrealistic need for perfection that makes them need to achieve it in order to view themselves as valuable or worthwhile.

Not much of a life, is it?

You always have the power to put your work in its place. Do a great job, but realize it is your *job* — not your world. Your identity has many facets, and it's all right if you have one or two or ten other things that matter to you as much or even more than your title and your place of employment.

Remember what Lisa Kruckeberg said. You only get so many trips around the sun.

At some point you have to ask if you are giving work more or less of your life than it deserves. If something is out of whack, remember what Lisa said. Time is finite. If your work isn't working for you, you can make changes that will still give you a rewarding career *and* an outside life. Reset it.

It's your life. How do you want to spend it?

CHAPTER 7

RESETTING YOUR (SOMETIMES) MISERABLE JOB

There comes a time when you pack up your talent and go. You apply for a new job, you get it, and you start a new adventure.

But do you always have to move on in order to reset?

What if you aren't ready?

What if you don't know what you want to do next?

What if there are financial considerations that can't be ignored? Or if there is so much going on at home that a job change is out of the question?

Is there any way to salvage a job or career that may be dragging you down? Maybe it's because the company is in turmoil, or because a new boss isn't all that great or your coworkers are nasty or negative, or because you've gotten bored.

You may have legitimate reasons for wanting to stay put. You've got too much invested. You're too close to retirement. You like your company, but you're getting bored with your actual job.

If your situation is not going to get better with the reset solutions in this chapter, open up to the possibility that reset, for you, may mean moving on. Sometimes you need a reset because your work*place* is the problem — not your work. You are entitled to enjoy what you do, and when you realize that the bad days are outnumbering the good, you need to take action.

But for many, there is the possibility of a reset at work, where you stay put, but you change what you can change. There are things you can do when your profession fills you with purpose, but your work environment doesn't. Here are some things you can do to reset how you feel about your job without moving on.

1. GO ZEN.

Mindfulness is the one thing that gives you ownership over your entire experience on this earth. When you are in the moment, you aren't obsessing about what is wrong or what might happen or what needs to change. Just be. Breathe. Stop worrying and start living. Peace is within you, but you have to nurture it.

2. STOP HATING YOUR BOSS.

That doesn't mean you have to force yourself to love a bad boss. It's probably not very likely to happen anyway. But fixating on a bosshole is only going to aggravate you, hike your blood pressure, stress you out, rob you of sleep, and make you miserable. Why give him or her that kind of power over you? I assure you, your bad boss is not expending that kind of time or energy on you. All bad bosses are temporary players in our lives. They move on, or we move on. The only way you are stuck with a bad boss forever is if you refuse to recognize your power to either deal with a bad situation or leave it.

3. LOOK AT WHAT YOU ARE DOING.

Try to give your brain the space it needs for clarity. Eliminate noncritical tasks and obligations. Stop cramming so much into your day that you don't get the time you need to get back in the game — or change the game itself.

Stop rushing. If that means leaving earlier, see how you might make that happen. Look at how you are spending your time to see if you're cutting things so close that you're increasing your level of stress. If you need more family time, find a way to create it by clearing a few things off your plate like housekeeping, yard work, or other time drains that can be outsourced. Yes, taking charge of your time may have consequences for your status in the office, but it may be the only way to keep both your job and your sanity.

I have helped so many people manage their time and focus to give themselves the ability to head home earlier. But if there is absolutely no way to make adjustments so you can be happier in your job, then you will need to make some bigger changes and, perhaps, leave.

Take breaks. Nobody is so important that they can't step outside for some fresh air or to have lunch. Doing this means your life is composed of more than just your daily grind. And when you feel that you have a little control over your time, your mind will begin to clear. You'll actually be more creative and productive.

4. CHERISH THE GOOD AND STOP FIXATING ON THE BAD.

How many conference calls, how many meetings, and how much administrative tedium can you stomach before it hits you that you aren't doing much of the work you love the most?

When you start to get frustrated, consciously focus on really enjoying the parts of your job that you do love. Chances are that you would still have to handle the calls and the unpleasant, bureaucratic stuff in another job.

On the flip side, when you're stuck doing the stuff you hate, tell yourself, "This is the price of doing what I love, so I'll gladly make peace with these obligations." Say it over and over again until you believe it.

I would *love* my work so much if all I had to do was write books and speak. But I don't get that luxury. If I'm being honest, my real job is marketing so that I can sell my books and get the speaking events that I love so much. It's just as important that I have conference calls, manage my website, and dive into other efforts as it is that I do a killer keynote. That's my reality.

So when you feel dragged down by the duties that you really don't enjoy, remember what a privilege it is to be able to make a living doing the work that you love — even though you don't get to do it 100 percent of the time.

5. CREATE TIME SO YOU CAN FOCUS ON WHAT YOU ENJOY.

If you take a more disciplined approach to your day, you can create time pockets that let you focus on the work you love most. Time management has always been a problem in the professional world, but these days, the issue is managing your *focus*.

Who can focus anymore? We have endless distractions. Our phones summon us when anyone texts or e-mails or calls, or when our calendar reminds us that there is an appointment coming up, or if there is big news or somebody posted a picture of their dog on Facebook. You can give up your life keeping track of all of the notifications you get, and you can become obsessed with checking your e-mails around the clock.

You do, however, have some power in this area. First, set some electronics boundaries for yourself. Turn off the notifications on your phone so you don't hear a distracting noise every time someone or some app wants your attention. Second, take charge of your calendar so you are consciously spending your time in a way that is most productive.

If you have eight hours in the office, how are you going to spend them? Write down your tasks for the day, then determine how much time each task should take. Deadlines are powerful tools for both time and focus management.

A great way to enforce a deadline is to set a timer. And good news! There is a timer with an alarm right in your phone. Siri — on my iPhone — is a big help to me. I say, "Tell me when twenty minutes is up," and she sets the alarm for me. I then focus on what I need to be doing so that I get the task done in twenty minutes. Usually, I make it. If I don't, I set another deadline. But I am always, always, *always* more productive when I'm using a timer than when I'm not. It is extremely helpful because it keeps me from checking Facebook or wandering aimlessly to different websites.

Take charge of your time and your tasks, and you will have more time to focus on the parts of your work that fulfill you and bring you happiness.

6. TUNE OUT THE NEGATIVITY.

I know it's hard sometimes, but you have to take charge of the things you allow to ruminate in your head. One way to start loving work again is to start loving work again. Write down the things that go right instead of fixating on the things that go wrong. Keep a log of what you are accomplishing so you can see visually that your contributions and your work matter.

Instead of being frustrated by small things, look at the bigger picture. Remind yourself that what you do matters to your company, your coworkers, and your customers.

When you feel the negative seeping in, tell yourself, "It ain't perfect, but look what I get to do."

7. DISENGAGE FROM NEGATIVE PEOPLE.

Gossip and negativity from others are toxic — period. You can have the best attitude in the world, but once you start listening to negative people rambling on in their doom-filled rants, it takes a toll. Negativity breeds negativity. When you keep hearing people complain about things, you will often complain with them or internalize what they are saying.

Don't go there.

Stop listening.

Tell yourself, "I am focused on positive things and I'm going to let go of the negative." If you don't, your mind will accept the poison. The negativity and cynicism of others can spoil your attitude, but only if you let it. Choose to deliberately neutralize the pessimists.

8. CHECK IN WITH DALE.

Often, the problem's not your job — it's the people. You're probably not going to be able to change the behavior of the people around you, but you may get a different result if you do a little work on yourself.

If you haven't read Dale Carnegie's classic, *How to Win Friends and Influence People*, read it. If you have read it, it's time to read it again. The book was first published in 1937, and it remains the best-selling self-help book of all time.

I'm just sorry I waited to read it until I'd just about been crushed by office politics.

I can't say enough about the wisdom of this book, or the impact it can have if you let it change your approach to dealing with others. It shows how to deal with people, how to win them over, and how to get them to change and respond. It's about *them*, not you.

It's amazing how people respond to the techniques shared in this book. The old adage "You'll get more flies with honey than with vinegar" gets to the heart of what makes people respond. It makes you effective because the people around you will like you and want to help you be successful.

Once you start practicing the Carnegie system, you will be shocked by how much easier it is to deal with people who have been difficult for you in the past.

9. CHANGE THE SCENERY.

A quick and easy visual reset can occur if you simply move your desk, change the paint in your office, or even redecorate your cubicle. Granted, it's not going to completely overhaul your emotions, but it's *something*. Add a picture of your happiest memory, a plant, an inspiring quote — anything that will bring your mind and your focus to a good place.

You can achieve another change of scenery if you volunteer for a special assignment or try for a different job. New locale, new people — whatever it takes to refresh your perspective.

10. TAKE SOME TIME.

Sometimes you just need a day off — or two — to chill out, own your power, and refresh your energy.

I've already mentioned my friend Joyce Duarte, who was the executive assistant to the managing editor of the paper in Jacksonville. Joyce had a theory about mental health days: If you are going to take one, take two. Two is more believable than one.

One time, she took two days, and when she came back, the executive editor of the paper asked her about her symptoms.

"Did it start with a scratchy throat?" he asked.

She assured him that it had. She then regaled him with a list of all of her other symptoms.

The next day, *he* called in sick with those very symptoms.

Right after that, his assistant called in sick with the very same fake illness.

And to cap it off, the managing editor called in with it as well.

All for an illness that had never existed in the first place.

Sometimes, you've got to take a day off. Or two.

While some companies may hate when a worker cuts out because of stress or job fatigue, others make a practice of giving personal days or extra paid time off because they know employees may need that time to de-stress and renew. According to researchers from Harvard and the National Institute of Mental Health, it's estimated that Americans take more than 1.3 billion mental health days each year for depression, anxiety, or stress. Researchers didn't specify whether the mental health issues were personal or work-related, but workers *are* stressed. A 2014 Gallup study found that 73 percent of Americans are unhappy about the amount of stress connected to their jobs.

Deciding to stay home — or relaxing somewhere else away from work — can give you the temporary power that you need in a situation where you may feel completely powerless.

11. ASK FOR WHAT YOU WANT.

When you are miserable and ready to go, why not ask your boss for the changes you need that would keep you in your job? It's either that or speak your mind in an exit interview when it's too late to do anything about it.

I learned this lesson when I was 25 years old. I'd always wanted to be a feature writer when I was in college, but when I went to find a job, the editor of *The Florida Times-Union* insisted I had to do hard news on the city desk for at least a year. I was a natural investigative reporter, but I still thought I wanted to be a feature writer. So after my year with hard news was up, I held him to his promise. I told him I wanted to transfer to features, and he transferred me.

I was miserable over there. I immediately missed the sense of urgency I'd had doing hard news, and I missed the people. I'd made a huge mistake and knew I had to find a job at another newspaper where I could work on a city desk.

When I told my mom that I was getting my resume together, she said, quite simply, "Why don't you just go ask for your old job back on the city desk?"

I didn't see how I could, but Mom said, "You have nothing to lose."

I went into Ron Littlepage's office and said, "I don't like what I'm doing. I'd like to come back to the city desk."

He smiled at me, said, "Okay," then stood up, walked over to the features department, and told the assistant managing editor that I would be returning to my old job on the city desk.

Happy Fawn went right back to where she belonged.

My point is that you may have more leverage or greater options than you think. Don't assume that what you see is what you are going to get. You won't know if you can create a better situation for yourself if you don't ask.

12. GO BACK TO CLASS.

When you are trying to figure out what to do with your job or career, you always have the option of doing an external reset that will make things much more tolerable in the office.

While I struggled with a horrible jerk of a boss in Denver and stuck it out at the job, I signed up for a screenwriting class at the University of Colorado.

I was instantly liberated.

Suddenly, I was immersed in the world of fiction. Nobody could tell me what to write, how to write it, or when to write it. It was so much fun, so exhilarating. I would come home and get to work. I'd spend my weekends writing my passion.

No, I never did get a movie produced from my efforts, but it was so therapeutic for me. Having that new, exciting outlet — and the challenge of a college class — reminded me that there was more to my life than my job. It gave me the time I needed to figure out what I wanted to do about my career.

So by all means, stretch. Learn something new. You can do something for pure enjoyment or take coursework that will set you up for a possible career change ahead.

13. TAKE CARE OF YOURSELF.

One way to give yourself the oomph to persevere through your workplace challenges is to hit the gym, go on a diet, minimize caffeine, alcohol, and nicotine, and do whatever it takes to honor your physical well-being. Make a good night's sleep a priority. And surround yourself with support. Lean on your friends as you figure things out. Doing this will help to minimize your stress and center you so you won't feel down or negative during the day.

It may not be a cure-all, but you don't know how much it will help until you try it. So begin by committing to a two-week regimen and see if feeling better about your physical self helps you to deal with your stress or unease about work.

14. IF IT'S CLEAR THAT YOUR AT-WORK RESET WON'T WORK …

If you've tried and you still aren't feeling the love for your work, it's time to start considering your options. Have Plan B ready. That means your resume is up to date and you have an idea of where you might want to go if you decide to make a change. There is absolute power in being ready. It doesn't take that much time. How long does it really take to redo your resume? Maybe a couple of hours?

If it's really time to go, GO.

If things aren't going to get better, they aren't going to get better. You still have all the talent that made you successful in the first place. Job hunting is difficult, but you can find another opportunity. Career transition may seem overwhelming, but take it one step at a time. It's not that bad.

A 2013 Harris study reported that fifty-five percent of working adults are interested in changing careers and about twenty-four percent are *seriously* wanting change. Only 14 percent of American workers are in their dream careers, the study reported.

It's interesting to look at the age breakdown of the people wanting career change:

- 78 percent of the workers in their 20s
- 64 percent of workers in their 30s
- 54 percent in their 40s
- 51 percent in their 50s
- 26 percent in their 60s

It's shocking to me that almost eighty percent of the twenty-somethings want something different — and more than half of the fifty-somethings are still wanting a change.

People want change for different reasons. Can I say without a doubt that it's because the respondents suddenly want balanced, deeper lives? Of course not. Maybe it's boredom. Or that the industry has changed. Or perhaps their career isn't all they expected it to be.

Regardless of the reason, if you are unfulfilled and things aren't going to get better, do something! You have permission to live your life your way. Do what calls you.

Gary Urso has spent the past year in a 500-hour, comprehensive program that will train him to be a professional hypnotherapist.

Interesting, right?

Especially when, for the past thirty years, he has been a successful divorce lawyer.

Gary's had a huge life reset over the past eight years. Eight years ago, he sold his waterfront home in Clearwater, Florida, got rid of his two boats, then downsized back into his first house, the 950-square-foot home he'd been using as an investment property for years.

He went from a $2,500 mortgage payment to no mortgage payment, and from a $500 electric bill to a $100 electric bill.

"I don't feel the least bit compromised in terms of quality of life," Gary says.

He is free.

For months, he said nothing to his friends, waiting to see if the hypnotherapy would hold his interest. It did. Now all of us are lining up and asking for the friends and family rate.

He is living *his* life, and he is alive.

15. HANG IN THERE.

I know what it feels like to experience that Sunday night anxiety before starting yet another week at a miserable job. It can look pretty bleak when you don't see a way out of your frustration and stress. I promise you, *there is a way out.* Either you can find a way to make your job work for you, or you can ready yourself to pick up, make changes, and move on.

It helps to know that you are in charge of your life.

Your relationship with your job — for better or for worse — is very similar to your relationships at home. You can't pack up and leave because you are miserable parenting a teenager, so you have to find a way to make it work. And your relationship with your husband, wife, or partner also has its highs and lows.

You know what they say about a good relationship? It's a lot of work. There are good days and bad days with your spouse or partner, with your screaming teenager, with your siblings and parents. It takes work to make those relationships work, and the same goes for your relationship with your job.

CHAPTER 8

GO DEEP

When I was a young reporter in Jacksonville, Florida, I would frequently disappear on the weekends to camp on nearby Cumberland Island National Seashore, an eighteen-mile barrier island off the coast of Southern Georgia, accessible only by boat. I'd ride the ferry out on Saturday morning, then take the last one back on Sunday evening.

"Back to reality," I'd say, sighing to the ferry captain as we headed back. I loved my job and my life in Jacksonville, but I always hated leaving that island. It had become my refuge.

I will never forget that bearded captain looking out toward the sun as it set so brilliantly over the marsh.

"*This* is reality," he said.

"Well, sure," I said. "But for most of us, this is an escape."

"Then most of you have it all backwards," he said.

I remember that moment so clearly because he was so right.

When it comes to living, most of us have it all backwards. We get lost in the chaotic world we humans have created, rather than grounding ourselves in the wonders of the reality that exists in spite of what humans have done.

The earth — that is real. The warmth of the sun — that is real. The freshness of the air — that is real. The love of family — that is real. Our connection with God — that is real.

But the stress of a job? The unkind thing someone said about you? National politics? World affairs? The new couch you think you need? Someone else's opinion of you? Are those things real?

Or are they just noise?

We busy ourselves with thousands of concerns that, in the end, will not affect our lives in a meaningful way.

Reset your reality to liberate yourself from the usual chaos of living.

YOUR SPIRITUAL CONNECTION

There is no way I can write this book without talking about spirituality. I will never tell you what to believe. But I will tell you to believe something.

"We are not human beings having a spiritual experience; we are spiritual beings having a human experience," wrote French philosopher Pierre Teilhard de Chardin.

If you buy that — which I totally do — you suddenly have the ability to lift yourself out of the fray and experience life — *really experience life* — as the learning experience it is. You can either leave this earth enlightened by all of the lessons from your experiences, or you can miss the whole point.

If you want to know the true joy and mystery of the life you are experiencing, let go and go deep.

Instead of getting lost in the drama of the moment, step outside of it and see it for the valuable learning experience it can be. Whether you're experiencing anguish or exhilaration, victory or defeat, love or loss, the whole point of the lesson is the lesson itself, because it will teach you who you are.

We are here to live, connect, and grow. Winning in this realm means we must fill our time with meaning and purpose. There are so many moments of challenge and adversity that push us to define our character with intention and mission.

You are a spiritual being having a human experience. Embracing that perspective is the ultimate personal reset.

Instead of seeing the intensity of the moment on a flat dimension of light/dark, happy/sad, win/lose, he said/she said, let yourself look at it from above. If you are a spiritual being having a human experience, why is this lesson playing out in this way? What are you supposed to learn?

Our work can become all-consuming and all-important, but when we take the larger, more spiritual perspective, we see that work can really distract us from our larger purpose of learning and growing.

Our work is not our sole purpose or our "soul" purpose for being on this earth.

By all means, love what you do, and do it with passion! But keep the stress of your work in perspective. It consumes so many people. I imagine that, when God looks at it, he sees we are spending a whole lot of energy on something that is ultimately meaningless in a spiritual realm. We don't get spiritual points for being good at our jobs — we get points for being good at our role in humanity. I'm sure God is happy if your job makes you happy, especially if you are developing your talents and helping others, but He probably isn't too worried about how far you climb that corporate ladder or how well any given project turns out.

Your purpose on this earth is to develop as a human being. Love your work, enjoy every possible aspect of it, but don't let it consume your opportunity to develop on a deeper human level. If past ups or downs in your job are getting to you, let them go. Do you think you'll get scolded in the afterlife for a bad performance evaluation or some big project that didn't go well? My guess is that God doesn't care about any of that. So if He doesn't, should you let it consume you?

I do think it matters when you hurt others to advance yourself in your work because that is a character issue. Work gives us endless opportunities to define ourselves with character and integrity — or not. We can face our work with either greed or generosity. With selfishness or selflessness. And what we choose to do shapes and defines our purpose here on earth. Our work gives us a chance to test, confront, and experience. Work is not a purpose, but it can be a *vehicle* to our purpose.

Are you achieving that purpose? Someone else may tell you that you need to do this or that in order to achieve your "potential," but you are the only one who can — and should — define your potential and how you want to spend your energy.

The larger question is always, "Am I achieving my *human* potential for the time I am here on earth?" If you are spending your time doing that, you are spending your time wisely. If you are focusing on things that are ultimately meaningless once it is time for you to leave this earth, then you are wasting your efforts.

Recalibrate. Reset. Go deep.

There is a peace that can exist inside of you, a real peace, a liberating peace that frees you. Life's distractions don't have to affect you on a soul level. You can choose this peace. But it will not come to you without you making this choice.

You can choose a path filled with personal mission and depth rather than expectation and inevitability. The second path is well-worn. Will you notice anything missing if you don't travel it?

What you allow into your head greatly impacts the way you experience your life, and you have control over that.

When you remind yourself that everything that happens is educating you and developing your soul, it is easier to disengage from many of your worries.

On a soul level, our daily dramas are simply meaningless.

That is a very hard awakening to embrace, but if you believe that you were brought here to live and grow and learn, and you have a spiritual component in that, you've got to realize that you probably obsess about a lot of things that aren't important to your larger self.

THE WORK ENVIRONMENT

It's not surprising that you might lose perspective when it comes to work because you likely spend at least forty hours a week there. You can't spend that much time immersed in anything without it influencing your frame of reference. There is a hierarchy that tells you in no uncertain terms who is more important and who is less important. You are told what you need to know, do, and, often, think. You are told when you need to show up and where you need to be. The culture governs your wardrobe and your tone. You deliver a work product that someone else dictates — even if you are working in a collaborative team environment. You are assigned tasks. Given priorities.

You work, then you get paid. And the more you fit into their culture — their reality — the greater your rewards.

When everybody is frantic over a huge deadline, you sense its immediacy and importance. It takes precedence over everything else.

You have to navigate the politics in order to move ahead, or you must come up with a survival plan when you've messed up. There are people you have to listen to, whether you like them or not. And you have to bow to their authority. Maybe even stomach their morals. Things often get a little muddy.

There is endless intrigue at work. What is going to happen to the company? How is new technology going to change things? Who is going to survive the layoffs? Why didn't you get that raise? How come they promoted that idiot? Doesn't anyone appreciate you?

There's sabotage. There's gossip.

The politics unfolds around you all day, every day.

So it all must be very important, right?

This environment, with all of its intrigue and activity, shapes your world because you are there in the middle of it. For hours and hours and hours. So we operate on the level of human experience and are distracted by this illusion of reality that we invite into our perspective.

Work paints one picture. The media certainly paints another, by telling us what we should look like, how we should think, and what we need to worry about.

I left a very long career in journalism with the realization that much of what we reported with such ferocity did not even matter. That is heresy for a journalist to say, but it is my truth.

News is rarely good, and that colors our view of what is real. Bad news can fill us with fear and anger that we don't have to experience if we tune it out. There is endless conjecture about things that ultimately won't happen. Things are exaggerated and blown way out of proportion.

I live in Florida and have to resist tuning in to premature weather reports that come ten days early telling me that a hurricane seems to be barreling right toward my house. People frantically rush to the local big-box store to load up on supplies, but two days later, the report changes and the storm turns and we don't hear anything more about it.

It all seems so pointless.

You truly do not know until a few days (and sometimes only a few hours) ahead of time, so why start worrying until it's time to worry? Just have your basic supplies on hand and, if it's time to worry, go buy more stuff.

The point is to be deliberate about the reality you choose to perceive.

Instead of obsessing about the coordinates of a hurricane that is ten days away or pondering whether

Congress and the president will agree on something by midnight tonight, go outside, breathe in some fresh air, and connect with that earthy reality that the ferry boat captain immersed himself in. And when you go there, go deep.

MULTIPLE REALITIES

I spent decades worrying about that "real world" that consumes most of us, and what did it get me? Anxiety.

And then it hit me.

There can be multiple realities playing out at the same time.

There is the reality in the news. There is the reality that the reactionary kooky bloggers present. There is the reality that you see. And then there is your individual reality, the one filled with fresh air, trees, beaches, positive thinking, good people, and all the happiness you invite into your life.

Which reality will you believe?

Which one will you choose to see?

Once I started seeing myself as a spiritual being having a human experience, an unbelievable calm opened me up to a much more intense, immediate relationship with God. That has given me a perspective that I feel called upon to share with others because I am convinced that they will be happier if they consciously decide what really matters to their reality — and what just doesn't belong.

I took 9/11 very, very hard. How could such a terrible thing have happened? How could a loving God allow it?

Two weeks after the tragedy, I ventured outdoors and went kayaking through Longboat Pass on the west coast of Florida. It's my favorite place to kayak because there is every color of wild turquoise and blue in that water, and it's magical. Not quite Tahiti or Bali, but as good as you'll get on the mainland United States.

So there I was in my kayak when I noticed something.

It was a beautiful day.

A magnificent day.

The most beautiful day I had seen in a very long time, if ever.

I stopped thinking of the tragedy and focused on what was in front of me. Blue and turquoise and aquamarine! And dolphins! And finally a striking red sunset! It was a perfect day.

Or was it?

Because if I had not gone out there that day, it would have been a terrible day. I would have stayed stuck in that traumatic place we all experienced. I would have been thinking about people who had died, their families, the terrorists who had killed them, and the terrorists who would like to kill me.

Yet there I was, vibrant, breathing, living, and immersing myself in a reality that could only be described as paradise. That was my day. That was my reality.

Could both realities exist?

YES.

Millions of people spent that very day still trapped in the dark reality that consumed us for so long.

But all of the people I saw at Longboat Pass that day were sharing that shining, stunning moment in nature.

There is truth in both realities. Both can exist at the same time.

But one hurts, and the other heals.

Is it a crime to choose the one that heals over the one that hurts? Are you burying your head in the sand or ignoring your human obligation by taking a time-out from the trauma? As we saw in the days, weeks, and months after that tough moment, there came a time when everyone moved on. We didn't forget. But we picked up and started living again. Individually, we have the ability to do that sooner rather than later.

You choose your reality and choose when it needs a reset.

Two people can go into the same exact situation with two completely different attitudes and have completely different experiences.

There are times when we are victimized by others, and times when we victimize ourselves. Either way, we are presented with opportunities to learn and grow. Others can shape our experience, but we control our reactions, thereby defining what winds up being real and meaningful to us.

People who choose positivity create a very different reality from those who always look for what is wrong. We can influence our experience by having a good attitude. There are dozens of books written about the "law of attraction," a guiding principle that I believe in and embrace. Put simply, if you expect good, you get good. If you expect trouble, you get trouble. If you expect lack, you get lack. If you expect abundance, you get abundance. You manifest what you expect. You can always reset your expectations.

You can practice something that I call the "law of dismissal."

THE LAW OF DISMISSAL

There will be times when unpleasant and painful things will happen to you. There will be losses, rejections, illnesses, hardships, and huge difficulties that put obstacles in your reality that you would love to ignore — but you can't. There will be people you have to deal with who will hurt or harm you. There will be times when you lose when you expect to win. Moments that you are in danger when you assume you are safe.

You cannot run from fate.

But you can control so much about what stresses you by taking charge over the realities you prioritize.

That means you ask the question, "Do you live to work or work to live?" If you want to be in the "work to live" category, you dial down the volume on work-related stress because work no longer owns you. It is a part of your life — not your life.

When you face other stresses in your life, ask whether they matter to your heart and soul — or not. If they don't, you can consciously minimize your emotional attachment to the situation. You still have to deal with the challenging situation, but you don't have to let it possess you.

Instead of passively reacting to what is on the plate in front of you, take time to really look at what you're facing. Closely examine what you are dealing with. How deeply do you have to dive into the situation? Can you control the degree of stress you experience? Is this something that has to be a part of your reality? If so, all the time?

Making the decision to choose your peace is a huge reset moment.

Life will throw chaos and crisis in your path. There will be conflicts and stresses so seemingly powerful that you get sucked into the vortex.

And yet there will be times when you have a choice to feel bad about those situations — or not. When you can acknowledge them, or go into intentional denial. If you emotionally shut them out, are you being weak or strong? Healthy or unhealthy?

Deciding what you invite into your life and what you don't starts with an understanding of who you are and how you want to live. You are not always in charge of what happens to you in life. In fact, there are many, many things that are beyond your control. But you are in charge of what you are going to spend your energy caring about. And, more important, you can control *how* you care about those things, and how much. That requires self-awareness and inner depth.

You can't delete a medical diagnosis from your life. But you can decide how you are going to face it, who you are going surround yourself with, and what you are going to do to learn and grow from the challenge. You cannot control what your body is going to do or how things will turn out, but you can greatly influence how you experience it.

You get fired. Your husband walks out. Your mother has a stroke.

Your biopsy comes back, and it is malignant.

There is no way you can get out of bed the next day and not know that your old reality is gone. Just remember, you do have some say over what your reality is going to be.

My close friend Debby Deacon is in terrible pain from

the bulging discs in her lower spine. We had dinner one night, and she must have stood up twenty times to get a moment's relief from the pain. It'll be weeks before she knows whether last week's agonizing injections fixed the problem. It's possible she will spend the rest of her life suffering from this. And it is just as possible that she won't.

Regardless, she is certain she will be okay.

"One of two things will happen," she said. "Either I will get better, or I will deal with it." The law of dismissal.

Her ability to cope and find a way to live with what is coming takes the stress out of the unknown for her. She is choosing her reality, controlling the outcome in a situation she cannot control. And that is power.

It's the same power you can have.

But it is hard to be optimistic all the time.

Other people will hurt you. Even people you love. Bad things will happen, even when you are a great person. You can try to figure it out, try to make sense of it, but sometimes, there just is no sense to be made. Our unease comes because we have a never-ending quest for fairness in this life. We strive for an equilibrium that does not exist. If it did, there would be no learning. Everything would be predictable. We would share the same expectations, values, and feelings.

What a boring world that would be.

You *are* going to get hurt in this life — many times. You will be hurt by circumstance, you will be hurt by people. You will be disillusioned by your naïve trust or your certainty that people and institutions will do what is right by you because you've always done right by them.

There is a fairly constant clash between our expectations and reality because we all expect different things from the same set of circumstances, and we all think and behave differently even though we are all sharing the same space. Life can't satisfy your sense of justice and my sense of justice at the same time every single time.

I hate to quote The Rolling Stones, but I have to because "You can't always get what you want, but if you try some time, you just might find, you get what you need." What a profound truth. Take an average of the good, bad, and ugly in your life, and you'll see that certain things balance out. You face your disappointments and obstacles and, in the end, you live, you survive.

How many times have you heard the cliché that "Life is unfair"? Well, is it? Because fair to you may be unfair to someone else, and vice versa. We generally see ourselves as the heroes in all conflict situations, and when things don't go our way, we feel victimized. We expect good because, in our minds, we give good. We expect truth because we give truth. We expect loyalty because we give loyalty.

But life is more than happy to slap us around and teach us again and again that we will face unpredictability and unfairness. We have the opportunity to step out of the drama and use the moment to go deep.

We create the reality that either grows or victimizes us.

We are here to learn. We are meant to be happy, but we must make the choice to create happiness, even when unhappy things happen. Our greatest growth often comes from our greatest pain. Use hardship to deepen your perspective, rather than make you wary or bitter.

You are not being punished — you are being taught. Sometimes, the lesson is obvious. Sometimes, it is just to show you how strong and resilient you are.

There are times when your mantra has to be, "I am going to stop trying to explain something that can't be explained." It will help you to graduate into the affirmation, "I have stopped trying to explain something that, ultimately, is meaningless."

That approach helps you define your reality and move you into a growth phase.

When you catch yourself in a dark loop, remember that what matters in your lifetime is depth of soul, not tit for tat. So when something goes wrong or is hurtful, do your best to step outside of it and view it from another perspective. Another reality.

We get so caught up in the theatrics of the moment, and it can make conflicts that are utterly meaningless seem critically important. Life makes much more sense when you remember that you are a beautiful person on a beautiful earth who is here to live a beautiful life. Things only get sticky when you lose that perspective and get sucked into the melodrama du jour.

When you can't shake it, you can always pull a Scarlett O'Hara. Faced with adversity, she'd say, "I'll think about that tomorrow" and "Tomorrow is another day." She always had faith that, regardless of how dark it got, another day would hold the solution. Did she have faith, or did she choose denial? Does it matter?

She chose her reality.

What will your reality be?

CHAPTER 9

ATTENTION RESET

It was 5:30 p.m. at the eyeglass store. Five of us were waiting impatiently for three technicians to sell or fix a bunch of glasses so we could get our turns. All I needed was one little screw for my sunglasses. There was so much tension in that store because so many exasperated, agitated people just wanted to get home.

I glanced outside, where a summer thunderstorm was beginning to move in. The wind picked up and blew through the trees, and I watched it, fascinated. I'd pick one tree, watching it shake and bend, then zero in on one branch, then one leaf on one branch. I watched that single leaf struggle against the wind, and I was lost in it.

Wow.

Five minutes later, my Zen moment was interrupted by the technician who fixed my glasses. But my brain was so rested — it felt like it had gotten a massage.

Everybody else in the room was still so irritated. Ticked off.

I am learning to be more mindful. It's a reset technique that can bring instant peace in a chaotic situation. I'm not great at it, but I'm way better than I used to be. And even short mindfulness exercises, like the one at Eyeglass World, end up changing my whole day.

I wish I could live in a mindful state where I am present in every moment, rather than being wound up about something in the past or future. I wish I could easily flip a switch to turn off the dialogue in my head when I'm thinking about people or work or whatever it is that's distracting me from truly being in the moment where I am.

But I am learning. We all are.

I used to think there was some sort of science to mindfulness that required extensive training from a monk or an academic. I now know that mindfulness is just taking the time to watch a single leaf in a storm.

UNCLOG YOUR MIND

Your mind is more than willing to clog itself up with thoughts and activity. That's the norm for most people. Thinking, obsessing, worrying, pondering, thinking, wondering, worrying ... the loop doesn't stop. And I do it, too, except I also make a deliberate attempt to be mindful and present every day.

I've coached people whose brains are so busy they become visibly stressed when I ask them to focus on being present — truly present — for one little minute. I set a timer and ask them to just slow down and focus on their breathing.

It's the classic Buddhist mindfulness exercise. You just say to yourself, "I am breathing in" when you are inhaling and "I am breathing out" when you exhale. That's all you focus on. Your breath.

But when I set a timer and ask those frenetic people to

slow down and do that for a minute, they become resistant and agitated. It makes them so uncomfortable, and while they laugh about how silly it is that they can't do it, they *really* can't do it.

It is painful for them to be in the here and now.

So I tell them to just try to do that one minute a day for a week, see if it gets any easier, then e-mail me back.

I've never gotten an e-mail back.

I feel sorry for them because I find mindfulness to be an extraordinary gift. It's comforting. It's grounding. It can instantly wipe out a stress loop from my brain.

The trick is to not make it into such a big deal. You'll get better at it when you stop making a big production of it. If you have trouble with it, lighten up on yourself. It's simply taking a mental time-out.

You can start by doing what I did with that leaf. Just choose a leaf and watch it. Sounds a little goofy, yes, but it is one way to stop thinking and start being. It's amazing how the gratitude seeps in once you escape into that space.

When I am out on the beach, I have to consciously turn off my brain. I look around, up, and then down. There is a wide expanse of earth and life — the reality I choose to immerse myself in outside of the "reality" of my daily grind. I feel a rush of calm and hope by just gazing at the sky and taking a long, deep breath. I often catch myself reaching upward, raising my arms in gratitude.

I am good at being in the moment for a few moments at a time. There are people who can spend hours in that zone, but I'm not there yet. What I am getting better at is returning to my mindfulness after a brain interruption.

My guess is that, on a three-hour beach walk, I'm probably mindful for about an hour. But I am constantly slipping in and out of it.

Mindfulness takes practice. You won't get fined if you aren't doing it right all the time, so don't let it frustrate you. Just enjoy it.

BE PRESENT

I once had a friend tell me that her therapist said her problem was that she was never living in the present. She gave her an assignment to be mindful for ten minutes each day.

"You are not in the present for ten minutes a day?" I asked, surprised.

"I'm never in the moment," she said.

"Not even during sex?" I asked.

"Not even during sex." She laughed.

"That would be the ten minutes I'd start with," I suggested.

It's a funny story, but it is, sadly, not unusual in the slightest.

We go through life without truly experiencing it because our minds aren't in the same place as our bodies.

Mindfulness doesn't mean you don't think about anything. It means you stop thinking about *every*thing and focus on what you are actually experiencing. I am mindfully writing this paragraph, enjoying the act of writing because it is one of my favorite things to do. I am perfectly capable of switching on the autopilot — but I don't because I love this work so much. When I finish this book, I'll be thrilled — and sad because I'll have to focus on something else. I'll miss you, my reader.

My dog Louie is 11 years old now – and he is the best dog I have ever had. I hate knowing that he is getting older, but every time I hold him, I feel love. I am mindful in all of our special moments because I know time is starting to run out. The day is coming when he won't wake me up with a kiss. So I am drinking in the love from my beloved, rescued pit bull every minute I can.

That's mindfulness. It's consciously deciding to throw yourself into the moment, rather than worry about what might transpire later on.

I once spoke at the Hilton Head Health Institute and was able to go through their program, a week of classes and healthy eating. We were fed the healthiest, low-calorie food, and we exercised all day.

Imagine our glee when, in the middle of a class, our instructor pulled out a bag of Hershey's Kisses and gave one to each of us. After a high-fiber, no-chocolate week, we could not believe our good fortune!

"Not yet," said Franny Gerthoffer, the instructor.

She moved us slowly through a mindfulness exercise that taught us so much about how much we miss by shoveling our food down our throats. Here is what she told us to do:

Look at it.

Smell it.

Bring it to your lips.

Close your eyes.

Put the whole thing in your mouth.

Then bite down on it.

Hold it.

Savor it.

Bite and hold again.

"After two tastes, you have experienced most of the taste sensation you are going to get," she said.

All of us knew that we could have devoured at least ten candies in the amount of time we spent savoring that one most delicious chocolate kiss.

How many meals have you consumed where you haven't really tasted a thing? Franny was so right. After a couple of bites, the thrill is gone — unless you are truly conscious of it.

That is such a great example of how we unconsciously go through life, so distracted by what's in our head that we forget to savor what is actually happening all around us.

When I'm in the shower, I'm not thinking about rushing off to the next thing I have to do. I allow myself to consciously feel and enjoy the sensation of the warm water on my body. I like the sound of the water as it cascades to the shower floor. I love how it feels to massage the shampoo into my scalp. Even if I have to shower in a hurry, I am *right there* in that shower, in that moment.

There have been a number of occasions when I've gotten caught in the rain. When it happens while I'm working and need to look my best, it's not good. But when it happens when I'm walking the dog or out on the beach or running errands, I have several options: I can rush to shelter, grab an umbrella, or get wet. It took me most of my life to realize that getting caught in the rain — and getting wet — can be quite a splash of life.

Cleansing, yes, but also freeing. There is a leap of spirit when you stop running from something that isn't all that scary. Sometimes, it's invigorating to just let go and submit. You stand out there in the rain, present in that moment, and it hits you that it is pretty freakin' amazing.

MAKE PEACE

Every summer, I wind up tubing down some of Florida's clear-to-the-bottom rivers, really special places that out-of-staters don't know about and most Floridians never bother to get to know. Every time I go to the Rainbow River, a menacing thunderstorm hovers nearby.

One time I went, and my friends were alarmed by the dark clouds moving in.

"Don't worry about it," I said. "It always does that, and it never rains."

Of course, on that particular day, the skies unleashed a violent, almost Biblical torrent of rain, thunder, and lightning so fierce that people were literally screaming in fear. There was nowhere to hide. We were all stuck out there in the middle of a river in a storm so menacing we could have been killed.

Okay, God, I thought. *If this is what you have in mind for how I'm supposed to die, I'm okay with it. It beats suffering a long, painful death. And since there is nothing I can do about this situation, I'm just going to stretch out in this inner tube and enjoy it.*

This same inner dialogue has served me well in several near-death moments.

Once I made peace with that situation, I leaned back and let the rain run over me, washing my stress away. And then something amazing happened. I smelled a fragrance from the woods that I'd never smelled. I heard sounds that I'd never heard. I felt so unbelievably alive, and I wasn't afraid. After all, there was nothing I could do but just live that moment the best way I possibly could.

When the storm finally ended, everybody was sharing how afraid they had been and how horrible the experience was.

I said nothing.

It was one of the most invigorating, fun, and inspiring moments of my life.

And I had that priceless experience because I was in the moment, living it and breathing it in for all the possibility it could hold — good or bad.

CHAPTER 10

DIVE FEARLESSLY

A few years back, I was on a kayaking expedition with a guide who launched us in turbulent conditions in the Ten Thousand Islands region of Everglades National Park and nearly got us all killed. He did not bring a GPS, instead relying on a compass, watch, and map to guide us through a three-day expedition to remote barrier islands in the Gulf of Mexico.

The first day, we were lost in fog so thick that we could barely see in front of us. Waves were splashing over the sides of our kayaks, and in every direction, the only thing we could see was the fog. His plan to compass-navigate us with a time and distance formula — one that was probably last used by Christopher Columbus — was a joke.

Darkness was setting in, and the four of us who'd trusted him to lead us were thinking the same thing: Odds were good that we would die out there. Naturally, we all found ourselves thinking of the recent high-profile news story of the NFL players who had recently drowned offshore in Florida after their boat capsized in the Gulf.

Oddly, I had a palpable sense of calm. I remember thinking that I should definitely be worrying about sharks because there were so many in that body of water. I remember also thinking of my family — how I wished I could tell them that I was not afraid in that moment. And I remember thinking how odd it was that I felt no fear at the thought of drowning.

I prayed silently.

God, if this is what you have in mind for how I am supposed to die, I am okay with this. It beats suffering like Mom has suffered for the last twenty years. But if this is not what you have in mind for me, you need to do something, right now. I seem to rely on that go-to prayer for all my near-death emergency situations.

Just then, we saw a tiny island of mangroves with just enough room above the high tide line for us to pitch our tents.

We were safe.

A few months later, for my 50th birthday, I did what every 50-year-old tends to do these days: I got a Groupon and went skydiving.

The instructor told me that when the time came, he would give me the signal to move back between his legs so he could clip my skydiving suit to his. We would then scoot to the edge of the plane's open door, where he would tap my shoulder and wait for me to give him the "okay" signal.

The moment came. I was clipped to him and at the open door when I got the tap on my shoulder.

I turned to him, and it was the first time I caught a whiff of his breath. Whoa! It smelled like he had just consumed a fifth of Jack Daniel's.

I prayed silently, saying once again, *God, if this is what you have in mind for how I am supposed to die, I am okay with it*. And then I added, *I will dive fearlessly into this and every moment for the rest of my life.*

And suddenly, I was free.

Obviously, I lived. But that line became the mantra that has given me the ability to dare to do just about anything. I remember walking out of the airport in Dubai and seeing everything in Arabic. I said to myself, *I will dive fearlessly into this and every moment for the rest of my life.* I said it again when I was traveling alone in India.

Gauge your own fear of death. On a scale of one to ten, how afraid are you to die right now? Once you shed the fear of death, you are free to live.

If you are full of fear, then it is time to reset.

KEEPING FEAR IN CHECK

When a plane starts to do the herky-jerky and other passengers start to panic, I just breathe out. If that is how I am supposed to go, fine. I believe there is more for me on the other side of this life, and if there isn't, I'll be dead and won't have much to say about it.

Worry and fear are often intertwined. You worry when your mind starts running wild with what-ifs. That escalates into fear when you are truly afraid of those what-ifs. There is a legitimate physical response as a result. Both emotions are vital — after all, you need to be alert in order to avoid danger or big mistakes — but you must try keep them in check.

I keep hearing all of these so-called statistics that 97 percent or 92 percent or 85 percent of what we worry about never manifests. You see numbers like that, and you know they're made up because how on earth can such things be measured? But there is an absolute truth to the notion that almost everything you worry about and almost everything you fear never even happens.

Why then are fear and worry so present in most people's lives?

"I have never lived fearlessly," said Caren Evans, an IT executive. "My mom's voice is always playing in my head. 'Don't do that. That's crazy. That's stupid ...' Living fearless — that's scary. I'm not attracted to that. Making a huge leap into the unknown is uncomfortable for me. Maybe if I were 85, I would do it. Might as well go crazy then, right? But not now."

Not now? Why not?

What is the worst thing that will happen?

What if you never make it to 85?

What if you let loose at 85 and suddenly discover how great it is? Then you've wasted 85 years and are too old to live the life you could have lived.

Life will give you endless opportunities to soar and endless opportunities to fall flat. You don't get advance memos telling you how every chance you take will turn out. You have to risk falling flat in order to soar.

That's living.

When you let go of fear, you find your freedom. And once you've found that, what is there to fear or worry about?

COMMON FEARS

•The unknown? If you don't know about it, why worry about it?

•Failure? You'll win some and lose some. If you aren't failing a little, you are nowhere near your limits.

•Rejection? Sooner or later, you will be rejected. Welcome to life.

•Bad health? You are going to get sick one of these days. Why are you worrying about it instead of relishing the good health you have in this moment?

•Financial disaster? Worry about this one, but get help to figure out how to manage it so that you don't have to worry constantly.

•Losing loved ones? Death is the sad price for life. It would not hurt if you weren't so blessed.

•Personal embarrassment? If you don't make a fool of yourself every now and again, you are acting like everybody else. Is that living?

•What your kids/spouse/boss/neighbor is going to do? You can't control everything. Keep it in perspective.

•What someone might say about you? Just be yourself. Listen to Wayne Dyer: "What other people think of me is none of my business."

You can fill your days with worry and fear or just go about your business and live your life. The one thing you know for certain is that you will have hard times and easier times. How they affect you is completely up to you.

I occasionally do pro bono speeches for local groups of people who are out of work and in transition. Many are in their 50s or 60s and are highly stressed because they are having real difficulty even being considered for jobs.

"Stop freaking yourself out," I tell them. "Is there anyone in this room who is in danger of living on the street or eating from a garbage can?"

Only once did someone raise her hand, and my heart

broke for her. She really was that close to homelessness. But none of the others were. They were miles away from such a thing, yet their minds were filled with worst-case scenarios that were paralyzing them with fear.

A man at one of these events raised his hand and told the group, "I can't leave the house. I try to force myself to apply for two jobs a day, but the rest of the time, I am in a complete depression."

That's a real shame because if you expect the worst, you tend to get the worst. Expect good things, and good things will come. I told him to stop wasting his days at home because the day will come when he is working a job and wishing he'd spent his time off better.

Either way, time will pass. You can either use your time or lose your time. Why not spend it doing things you enjoy with people you love?

I love this quote: "Everything works out in the end. If it hasn't worked out yet, then it's not the end." I wish I could tell you who said it, but I've seen it attributed to five different people, including somebody named "Anonymous."

Regardless, the point is the truth in the quote. Everything will make sense when it finishes playing out. There is not much to fear when you have faith that everything is going to work out in the end.

RISK IT

Most people don't stray far from their comfort zones. When I interviewed more than 300 great leaders for four of my books, I kept hearing one thing over and over again: If you want to succeed big, you must embrace risk.

Most people are afraid of risk because they don't want to fail. And that limits them professionally.

But personal risk is just as important.

That's why resetting your life can alter its course.

I know a woman who is in an absolutely miserable marriage with a man who is a verbally abusive jerk. They have a child together and literally scream their way through year after terrible year. She admits she is turning into someone she is not proud of, engaging in regular screaming matches that are making their daughter a nervous wreck.

"Leave!" I've said many times.

"I can't afford it," she says. "And I need him to pick her up after school because I don't get home until late."

I can't figure it out. She's making almost $50,000 a year. How can that not be enough to support a mother and child — especially since her husband would have to kick in something for child support?

If he died, she'd find a way. She'd have to.

But to her, their abusive, dysfunctional, and destructive situation is a known quantity. Even though her soul is dying in that environment, it works for her because it's predictable. Predictably awful, but predictable. She doesn't like what it's doing to her daughter, but she is convinced she has no choice.

But of course she does have a choice.

Don't blind yourself to other possibilities.

No one owns you but you. You and you alone choose the path you will travel, so if it feels wrong, you have the power — and the right — to make a change, to choose another way. But expect to encounter twists and turns and rocks in your way, and moments where you feel like you have reached a dead end, no matter which road you choose to follow.

Don't overthink it.

If you are living — really living — it'll all work itself out in time. It may not go exactly the way you planned it, but there will be a way to get where you need to go if you just go with it.

You have always had the ability to be powerful. It just takes a while to grow into it and learn how to use it. You have the power to make choices in your life, the power to tell others what you will and won't do, the power to set timelines. You can stay or go. You can conform or resist. You can relent or fight.

There will come a point when you will be ready to stop being victimized by life, and you will then begin to reconnect with your inner power. When you are moved to make changes because you find yourself in a desperate moment, you will draw on that power to begin your reset and take charge.

Do this in your own way.

Years ago, I worked for some extremely demanding people who knew how to push every button I had and make all of us feel insecure and miserable.

One of my colleagues left for lunch — and never came back. She hadn't even looked for another job but was confident she'd find something, which she did. The rest of us took our time sending out resumes, giving notice, and suffering as we continued to show up and attempt to function in that terrible office, all because we were trying to leave the way we were "supposed" to leave. Eventually, we found our power, too — well, most of us did. More than twenty-five years later, one member of our gang remains, still feeling unappreciated and still being mistreated.

People have the same range of responses when dealing with difficult relationships. Some quit too easily. Some wait it out, knowing something isn't quite right. Others will endure every kind of abuse.

Why do people stay in toxic situations?

Lots of reasons. Somebody who has a spouse with a terminal illness is less able to pack up and leave a bad workplace. Someone with an unstable job may feel less able to walk out of a bad relationship and thrive on his or her own. Life presents any number of circumstances that can make it difficult for us to exercise our options.

But the biggest excuse for inertia is fear.

Legions of people will endure endless abuses at work or in relationships because they are frozen in place, afraid that they won't be wanted elsewhere or won't be able to be successful in another environment.

They have every right to dive fearlessly into every moment of their lives, yet they don't do it.

WHY HOLD BACK?

Once you realize you don't have to fear your death, there is not a whole lot left to worry about.

The good thing about getting a little older is that you get to look back at all the good and bad that has happened in your life and see how everything seemed to fit together, as if it were planned that way. Something good comes from just about every bad thing, but it takes a while for all the dominoes to fall into place, and for you see the big picture of how everything worked out.

Think about the negative things that occurred in your life ten or more years ago. If X hadn't happened, then Y wouldn't have happened, and then Z wouldn't have happened. All of those things led you to where you are now, either in a good place already or taking steps to a better place.

Once you realize that adversity often leads to reward, you're free to take risks and try things, confident that what happens along the way is going to be the lesson you are supposed to learn. That doesn't mean you're completely fearless, but once you have faith that everything will work out, fear no longer holds you captive.

I'm not completely fearless, but there is much less fear in me now than when I felt I needed to try to control outcomes. At some point, I learned that growth comes when you *can't* control the outcome. You hit obstacles, but you refine your skills and learn how to get around them. You encounter a challenge and keep moving. That is growth.

Life really is an out-of-control experience — if you're living it right. If you hang on tightly, trying to ensure a positive outcome at every turn, you are never in the discomfort zone long enough to learn what you're really made of. You are missing the downside, where you swing and miss and suffer for it. You're also missing the upside, where you grow into a stronger, smarter, and deeper person. If you believe you are here to learn, don't cheat yourself out of the best lessons right in front of you. Those lessons are always rooted in discomfort.

And have confidence that you know what you need to know in order to make everything work out in the end.

No matter what happens. No matter how ugly it seems to get. You have the skills to know when something is wrong, when something needs to be adjusted — and then you have the ability to step back, get information, and analyze what you need to do.

What if you were suddenly forced to change everything in your life? Could you adapt? Would you dive in fearlessly, or would you let fear shut you down?

Steve Garnaas and I miraculously caught up with each other on a trip to Missoula, Montana. I hadn't seen him in a couple of decades, but I'd known him since my earliest days as a reporter in Jacksonville, Florida, when he was a great reporter who was drowning in alcoholism. By the time we both wound up as reporters in Denver several years later, he was sober. A different man.

The sober version of him looked good — happy. He'd found his rhythm, but then everything changed when he made a huge, career-ending reporting error that required a front-page correction in *The Denver Post*. He wonders if, on some level, he was sabotaging himself into getting fired because there was so much upheaval at the paper.

In his gut, he knew better things were coming.

"I knew it was divinely intended for me to move on to something else," he said.

But what? He'd been a professional all his life, but he suddenly found himself driving an airport shuttle van for six months until he got a customer service job with an airline. He was getting half the money he used to make, so he stayed with friends, sold his Jeep, and started cycling and taking the bus. He was forced to downsize his perspective, and he did it with absolute optimism. On his days off, he would use his flight benefits to travel the country and see old friends.

Four years ago, he became a flight attendant.

"I absolutely love doing that," he said. "I have maintained an 'attitude of gratitude' by staying focused and keeping a positive state of mind. I trek forward one day at a time. Certainly, there have been times of self-doubt and self-pity, but they never kept me down very long. Since walking out of that newspaper fifteen years ago, my life has been filled with the most meaningful and character-building times. My experiences were never life-threatening. My health has been very good.

"It's all good. It really is."

The thing I love most about Steve's story is his ownership of what went wrong. He never tried to hide it. He owned it, learned from it, picked up, and moved on, always finding the upside to his growth. He has never tried to sugarcoat what happened, only process it and grow from it. Why be embarrassed? That only prolongs your agony. Embrace all of your experiences for their lessons. We only continue to learn if we continue to open ourselves up to it.

There are people who never recover emotionally from the rejection and embarrassment of getting fired, jilted, passed over, or pushed aside. Their emotional experience is excruciating, but reliving it just keeps them mired in unpleasantness.

Steve's story shows how, when you buck up, you can get past the emotion and dive into possibility rather than fear and anger. I would never have predicted he would become a flight attendant. No one would have. But instead of wallowing in what went wrong, he turned it into something very right.

POWER OVER FEAR

Fearless living is not an absolute. Of course, there's something out there that *will* scare you. But you have the ability to overpower your fears. Yes, fear has a strong physiological component. If someone pulls a gun on you, you are going to feel immediate, intense fear, a rush of adrenaline and, probably, an innate response for flight. But you can generally manage most of your fears by breathing through them and calming yourself down with perspective.

So look at what you are doing and decide whether you can embrace a little more discomfort.

"My source of fearlessness comes from naiveté," said Laura Schwieterman, marketing director at Bayer Healthcare. "Thinking back on the courageous decisions I made in life, I made them because I was truly naïve to the downside. Isn't that also true of children? They are born fearless because they don't know better. Is there a lesson somewhere in there?"

Uh, yes.

JoAnn Salazar told me, "My parents raised a brood of fear-filled children. I have always lived my life weighing one fear against the other." Which is scarier? Going to the top of a high building or missing the experience? She was terrified of the Royal Gorge Bridge in Colorado, so, instead, "I rafted the Gorge — eight times," she said. "So I guess for some of us, it's a matter of balancing choices."

You don't have to force yourself to don a skydiving jumpsuit and roll out of an airplane or climb into a whitewater raft and push through Class IV rapids. The point is for you to do what you want to do in your life without letting fear stop you.

Dycie DeCambra has her own mantra on this topic: "If it's not worth a good story, it wasn't worth it."

And there you have it.

We are all just amassing material for our life stories. How do you even know that you are alive if you don't have a few amazing stories that no one else but you can tell?

If you're meant to die in whitewater rapids, you'll die in whitewater rapids. You don't have to cast all caution aside — don't be stupid on purpose. But don't stop yourself from daring to do what you deep down want to do. Calculate the odds, decide whether they are in your favor, and then take the plunge.

And feel free to take my mantra with you because it *will* help.

I will dive fearlessly into every moment of the rest of my life.

CHAPTER 11

FORGET PERFECTION

I will often ask people in my audiences if they are perfectionists. Many raise their hands — some proud, some sheepish.

What a hard life! If everything has to be perfect, how can you get anything done?

Imagine having to fix something every time you look in the mirror. Or having to always say the right thing. Or having to catch every speck of dust, every smudge on the wall, every streak in the glass at home.

And at work? How can you always deliver perfection when you are expected to deliver so much?

Salvador Dali famously said, "Have no fear of perfection for you'll never reach it."

Why is it that some people will literally starve themselves for months preceding their wedding so they can be thin, beautiful, and perfect? They spend the rest of their lives wondering why they don't look as good as they did on their wedding day. Well, I think they should *gain* twenty pounds so that, for the rest of their lives, people will say how great they look in the present.

There is no perfection anymore. So many senior executives have told me that this world moves way too fast for perfection or 100 percent certainty in decisions.

Perfectionists like having everything nailed down. It's comforting in its own way. But it's just not possible in life or in work.

Most companies appreciate the leader who makes a decision, knows what might go wrong, quickly sees where the problems are, and is ready to recalibrate and fix things as they go.

Those recalibrators are valuable leaders who move ahead.

Can you become a recalibrator in your personal life?

Legions of people are stuck in a rut of perfectionism. It stresses them out and steals time they could use for other things, like new projects or time at home.

And really, what *is* perfect? I don't know if I have ever written a paragraph that I couldn't improve. But doing that would impede my ultimate goal. I'd rather finish the book than have to continually rewrite the same paragraph, striving for that elusive perfection.

WHY PERFECTIONISM?

Perfectionism is often fueled by fear and a need for control. Perhaps there is a fear that anything less than perfect equals failure or a fear that less than perfect performance will expose the inadequacies the perfectionist thinks he or she has successfully hidden. The control element is especially pronounced when the perfectionist enters management and can't let go of control because, in his or her eyes, anyone else will mess it up. They make fabulous micromanagers.

And we all know that micromanagers are terrible leaders.

There are also perfectionists who turn on the obsessive-compulsive disorder faucet and can't turn it off when it comes to work. Perfectionism can be a compulsion.

If you are the kind of perfectionist who won't let go because you hear a voice inside saying, "Not. Good. Enough," relax. There is hope for you.

Affirmations will be a valuable tool for you (see Chapter 14), but here is a quick summary: The more you repeat something, the more it becomes your reality. The brain lets you tell it what to think, and repetition programs that thinking.

MANTRAS

Once you realize that perfectionism is actually holding you down and stressing you out, you can work to grow out of it. You do have to make the choice to reset. And it's easy if you repeat the following mantras over and over again for several weeks.

1. "I choose excellence over perfection."
2. "I am confident in my excellent work."
3. "It's okay to let go and move on to the next thing."
4. "I know when to let go."
5. "I'm getting so much more done now that I'm over my need for perfection."
6. "I've let go of so much stress now that I realize that I don't have to be perfect."

Just say those lines repeatedly until you notice the stress lifting. You can be just as successful — if not more successful — by embracing excellence over perfectionism. The reward is less stress and more time.

When I was an undergraduate, I went to a professor and asked if he could give me some extra credit. I was two points from an A, and I didn't want to blow my 4.0 average.

"You have a 4.0 average?" he asked.

"Yes."

"Well, I'm going to bust that average. You obviously aren't having any fun. Ordinarily, I would just give you the two points. But you need to get a B for a change."

I was furious, but the strangest thing happened after that B appeared on my grade report. The pressure was off. I could get an A *or* a B, and life would go on. In the meantime, I could start going to games, going camping, and staying out late with friends.

I could start living.

I never looked up that guy and thanked him, but I owe him a lot for that lesson. Especially since no one — not one single person — has ever asked me what my grade point average was in college. It did not matter one bit whether I had a perfect report card or not.

Come to think of it, no one ever asked me what my "chair" was in band. Or my time in my slowpoke triathlons.

Because, really, who cares?

So quit being perfect, already, and be excellent instead.

STOP STRUGGLING

There are so many times in life when you want to deliver, but you can't. It's not a question of perfection — it's a challenge of survival.

"You weren't your usual self up there," a colleague

told Marie Quintana, minutes after she had given a major speech to hundreds of fellow executives at a leadership conference.

Somebody had the nerve to say that?

Marie's father had died a week earlier, and they were very, very close. Someone had the nerve to criticize her?

"I wasn't myself up there? How could I have been?" she told me later. "But I showed up. I. Showed. Up."

Marie is president of Tu Familia Inc., which connects Latino communities globally through innovative mobile apps, and she is a former senior vice president at PepsiCo.

She shared that story with me right after my mom died. It helped me to forgive myself for those moments when I was not able to deliver my very best — even though I desperately wanted to. I was showing up. I was trying.

No matter how brilliant or savvy you are, there are times when you have a difficult run or a streak of bad luck that has a force of its own. You can either fight it and lose, or step out of it and catch your breath.

There will be moments when your challenges are so profoundly painful that all you can do is keep showing up. There will be times when so many things go wrong, they just wear you down. Sometimes, the cause is external. Sometimes, it's burnout. You can feel defeated or worn out by big things or little.

When those moments hit you, just keep showing up until you feel you are ready to reset.

Retired General Claudia Kennedy, the first female three-star general in the U.S. Army, presented this idea to me long ago when we were talking about those overwhelming moments in life. She taught me that you can't be a superstar every day. "Sometimes, I have to say, 'Look, stop struggling so hard. Just do some minimums for a while. Get through this bad period," she said.

She wasn't advising anyone to slack off. She was saying that there are times when you have to regroup and recharge. And sometimes, the only way you can do that is by deliberately easing the pressure you put on yourself by delivering a little less.

You can only hyper-perform for so long before you need a recovery period. It's not permanent, and it's not career defining. It is just a recharge moment that enables you to gather the energy you will need to hyper-perform again.

I have seen people hit the wall hard and then work even harder to force stellar results when they would have served themselves far better by taking a breather, recovering, and then going back at it.

That's why we have vacations.

That's why, when the pressures at home get a little much, a day at a spa is especially therapeutic.

Or why so many people take an occasional sick day when they aren't really sick.

That's why, when your loved one is in the hospital and you refuse to leave their side, a coffee break or a night in your own bed is like a Godsend.

There comes a moment when you must take a time out. You have to be able to release the pressure valve every now and again. And it's amazing how much better you can perform when you slow down and take that deep breath.

It was a really bad day for me several years ago when

two huge contracts fell through. I sat at my desk, trying to figure out what to do next, when Suzann Clark — a whiz at sales — told me, "Get out of here. You're done for the day. Get on your bike."

So I did. I cycled out to the beach, angry and totally in knots for the first hour. But once the workout had exhausted my resentments, I slowed down, cycling next to the Intracoastal Waterway as the sun did its diamond dance on the water and dolphins played offshore. My anger left me. I started the next day refreshed.

Had I not jumped on my bike, I would have stayed at my desk and not had a single fresh idea. If I hadn't ended that day with something positive and hopeful, the next day would have been born out of frustration instead of possibility, and I would have spent most of it fighting my way out of my funk.

By the end of that week, I had landed two really big speeches. And a month later, I got the call that one of the contracts that had fallen through was suddenly a go.

Sometimes you may think you're swimming in defeat, but you really aren't.

A time-out is a great reset moment. Math and science teacher Gale Postlewait has used that knowledge plenty with her sixth-graders for most of the past twenty-one years. There comes a point when even the kids need a reset.

"That's it!" she'll say, then open the back door to her classroom. It opens to an expansive field, and she has the kids run out to the fence and back. Or do some calisthenics. If it's raining, she takes them to the gym for relay races.

"Just ten to fifteen minutes of physical activity out of

the classroom, and then we go back," she said. "It's better than me yelling at them. They come back, settle down, and get to work."

You don't need to be a sixth-grader to benefit from that lesson. Sometimes you have to walk away in order to reset your brain.

"We have to know when enough is enough. We have to stop and take that break, then go back and persevere," Gale said.

On those days when everything is — or just feels like — a bust, push the reset button. The universe will not let itself be forced. Sometimes you have a run of bad luck or misfortune. That's how it goes. The best thing you can do at those times is extract yourself from that vortex and busy yourself with something else that makes you appreciate what you have. Then you can revisit your situation with fresh energy.

You can't force the universe, so stop trying.

Forget perfection.

Sometimes, you can only show up and do your best.

Sometimes, you need to deliberately slow down and do the minimum.

And sometimes, you just have to get on your bike and roll.

CHAPTER 12

REFRAMING YOUR COMPETITIVE MINDSET

I did quite a few triathlons when I was younger. Notice I say I "did" those triathlons — not *competed* in them. Quite honestly, my race times were so laughable, I'd register under a fake name in case my performance happened to be published on the Internet.

When I was living in Colorado, the events usually started in reservoirs or swimming pools. They were so civilized. I loved those events, loved the feeling of working out every single muscle.

But right after I moved back to Florida, I entered the Siesta Key Triathlon in beautiful Sarasota. What a spectacular morning at the beach!

And then ...

it turned ...

barbaric.

I was kicked in the head — hard — by three different swimmers. I was shoved out of the way by a guy in the transition area.

Why would I want to spend my Saturday morning getting kicked and shoved — or mingling with people who thought it was okay to kick or shove others — in order to get ahead?

I was in it to enjoy the event, the camaraderie, my fitness and endurance, the nature, and the moment.

But others were there to win — by any means necessary.

It made me wonder, if they win, then what? Was all the kicking and shoving worth it?

As you center yourself on your new course, step back a bit and think about how competition and perfectionism can drag you into situations that consume your emotions and time in exchange for a reward that is, in the end, meaningless.

I've seen people desperate to look better than their arch-rivals from high school at school reunions thirty-five years later, second wives competing to be better than the wives who came before them, people flat-out lying and selling their souls to score a few points at work. The list of crazy competitiveness goes on forever.

Think about the things you compete for in your life. There are so many situations where we push ourselves to stand out and be better than others. And some of it can be pretty silly. What do you compete for? Money? Status? Respect? Material wealth? Beauty? Promotions? Prestige? The thrill of the win or the joy of the fight? The satisfaction from a job well done?

The end rewards of competition are fine *if they translate into personal happiness.* But if you're stressing yourself out with competition for the wrong reasons, if it's draining your energy and the sacrifice is hurting you rather than helping, then it might be time to rethink what you're doing.

Some people fight to win because it makes them feel good to be "better" than their rivals. If that's you, remember this: Time will pass and eventually someone will be "better" than you are. Healthy competition involves teamwork, self-improvement, learning, and enjoyment. Isn't it "better" to feel your greatest satisfaction when you've pushed yourself to deliver your best?

And if you win on top of that, great.

But if you don't win, are you a loser?

You tried. You grew. You *did* something.

MISSING THE POINT

I once cycled from the Grand Canyon to Mexico with a good friend who was in such a rush, she didn't stop at a single overlook in that crown jewel of our national park system.

What did she win by getting to the campground first?

The knowledge that she'd done it faster than the rest of us? Sure.

But did she really win? She missed the entire Grand Canyon, after all!

Remember, the fun is out there while you travel your path — not just when you finish what you're trying to achieve.

With rare exceptions, there are always people who are smarter, faster, savvier, or more accomplished than you. Was the winner of the 1997 Siesta Key Triathlon the greatest athlete in the world? Of course not. So what did those head-kicking, people-shoving athletes win on that gorgeous morning? A personal best, maybe. But what did they lose in the process?

I'm all for competing against your own standard to achieve a personal best. But you don't have to step all over everyone else to be excellent. Just be great at what you do.

I was always shocked by the nasty internal politics at my first job at a small daily newspaper because people were willing to be unabashedly cutthroat. The knives were out!

In one especially juicy episode, a male feature editor was secretly recording the telephone conversations of the female city editor. Another female editor heard about it and secretly sneaked into the wire tapper's office, stole a cassette tape out of his recorder, and put it under the door of the publisher's office with a nice note.

At the same time, additional gossip constantly circulated, smearing other editors as wife-swappers or druggies. Such intrigue! All in an effort to rule that tiny little rag.

Unbelievable!

I can't tell you how many times I have watched people kill themselves trying to be the best among a bunch of mediocre people.

The problem with competing against others is that the others are setting the bar. If you are surrounded by great talent, odds are that the bar will be raised higher. But it can just as easily drop lower. Either way, the standard is artificial, and it's set *for* you.

So set your *own* standards. Perform because you are a performer. Excel because you are excellent. Deliver because it's in your DNA to deliver. This approach gives real perspective as you reset because it helps you set a more authentic, less stress-driven course that matters to you.

Years ago, I was cycling the Copper Triangle in Colorado, a 78-mile road bike ride over three mountain passes. I was leisurely climbing the first pass when a woman tried to zip past me, announcing, "On your left."

I sized her up and knew I was faster, so I just sped up and didn't let her get in front of me. (Childish, I know. I was 32.)

About twenty minutes later, there she was again.

"On your left," she said kindly.

I sped up again.

Twenty minutes later, I heard her voice. Again.

"On your left," she said in a very sugary tone.

"Are we going to keep doing this all day?" I asked her.

"Yes," she said.

So we started riding together. That whole day, we rode so hard and fast — she wore me out.

"You exhausted me," I told her.

"You exhausted me!" she answered.

We realized that, together, we had cycled harder and made each other stronger. After that, we probably cycled at least ten thousand miles together. Sure, we were competitive, but only because we could tease each other about our silly competition.

Riding together was so much better than trying to outride her.

What was I going to gain by not letting her pass me? Why did I feel the need to prove that I was faster and stronger than a stranger? Did it make me better than her?

Of course not!

And look at the friendship that came about when I stopped competing against her and started competing just to elevate my own performance. We were both much stronger training together.

WINNING ISN'T EVERYTHING

When you don't have to win, you can slow down and enjoy the scenery.

Competition can definitely inspire or prod us into excelling and achieving at a higher level, but be sure to set your boundaries and keep it in check so you aren't winning at the wrong thing. Competition is so enmeshed with insecurity and jealousy, two attributes that do nothing to develop us as human beings. There is no crime in winning the promotion or the perk or the award or the race. But there is a crime in stepping over others — or kicking them in the head — to get what you want. It's just not worth the bad karma that comes with it.

I am constantly shocked by what I have been told about office politics at certain companies. It's brutal at the top, brutal in the middle, and brutal at the entry level. The jockeying can be endless and the tactics vicious. If you have to stoop that low to move ahead, you have to ask yourself if the end result is even worth it.

We create ridiculous competitions and rivalries. Aside from the obvious and usual competition at work, people make themselves crazy over really stupid things. I remember my neighbor getting so mad when she was slighted for the garden of the month award. And then there are the competitions to look the youngest or be the thinnest. Or to have the biggest houses or the fanciest cars or the most exotic vacations. I've seen so many friends pushing their children, wanting them to be "better" than their friends' kids.

What does any of that insanity add up to?

It adds up to a life of comparison that diminishes your spirit if you choose to play the game.

Years ago, a colleague taught me a much better way to engage. It makes excellence the reward and eliminates feelings of rejection or loss.

Randy Loftis taught me to set goals that other people could not control. Instead of having a goal to win a Pulitzer Prize, he taught me to shoot to do Pulitzer-quality work. You may not be able to control the outcome, but you can control the output.

Do your best, and then keep everything in perspective. Years ago, I interviewed an executive from Procter & Gamble who shared with me what she told herself to keep things in perspective. Remember this concept, because it helps to keep the commotion, challenge, intrigue, and politics in check.

"We take everything so seriously, but we shouldn't," said Barb Hartman, the former vice president of customer business development at P&G. "I used to have a boss who said, 'Let's remember: We sell toilet paper.'"

CHAPTER 13

FACING LIFE

Rest assured, every crisis ends. It just does.

Sooner or later, the day comes when something *doesn't* go wrong. Then there is another good day. And another. All you have to do is keep getting up. Time is your friend.

I learned that years ago. Every crisis ends, and then when you look back on it, you see that everything fell into place as it should have. Everything led you to where you were supposed to go.

That was a lesson that repeated itself for me many, many times.

But a year did come when I was trapped in a tsunami of loss, death, crisis, and turmoil. It was *so much* crisis in such a short period of time. I felt the ripple effects for a long time afterwards.

Time went by, and things were still hard. Even when it seemed quiet, even when things seemed calm, I would once again be swept away in another giant wave of chaos. Time seemed to pass so slowly. For some reason, it just didn't seem to me like my crisis was ever going to end. I just couldn't face life.

In the meantime, I needed to find a way to get on with

life, in some fashion. To force myself into normal-ness, if even just a little bit.

That year took everything I had in my arsenal — and numerous other coping skills I hadn't tried. I took notes during all of this and now present my coping strategy here as a go-to checklist for you to use if you should ever be swept up by your own personal tsunami.

HOW TO COPE DURING A CRISIS

1) Cry. Sometimes, crying is all you can do. Just let the pain wash through you. Feel it. But know when the time has come to buck up and turn to other coping skills that will help you put yourself back together.

2) Pray. Pray. Pray. Do this in your own way. You've heard, "Let go, let God"? Back when I wasn't sure what I believed, I thought that line was a total cop-out. I felt like I should be able to fix everything by myself. Then I tried letting go. When I am overwhelmed, I just hand it over to God and start thinking about something else. Everything seems to fall into place. If you aren't sure how to connect with your spirituality, just slow down and look inside yourself. The three easiest prayers are "Please," "Thank you," and "Help." Don't listen to other people reciting the rules you need to follow in order to do your spirituality right. Define it for yourself. It's all right there inside you.

3) Feel gratitude. *"Imagine how happy you would be if you lost everything in your life — and suddenly got it all back again."* Best fridge magnet ever, right? When your mind starts running through an endless loop of despair and negativity, you can stop it by reading your personal gratitude list. Include everything and everyone: the people you love, your animals, friends, favorite places, your safety, your home, your health, sunrises, sunsets, your favorite physical activities, and all your memories. No matter how hard things get, you are still blessed and rich in life.

4) Use affirmations. Science backs this up. Affirmations are powerful tools to help you reprogram your brain and reset your emotional course. The catch is, you've got to be motivated to say them and in a receptive enough mood to hear and process them. Affirmations work, but only when you are ready to work them.

5) Exercise. It's like medicine. Exercise boosts your endorphins, the chemicals that join the receptors in your brain to reduce the perception of pain and trigger positive emotions. The euphoria you feel after a workout is said to be similar to morphine — without the morphine. Exercising reduces stress, anxiety, and depression. It improves self-esteem and helps you to sleep. All of which can help you heal.

6) Journal. Be your own therapist. Ask yourself questions, think about them, then journal your answers. This gives you time to process your thoughts in a safe place. If you can't figure out what questions to ask to move you forward in your situation, buy a workbook on anger or grief or career crisis or whatever you are facing. There are so many to choose from.

7) Ask your friends for help. Some friends intuitively know what you need and are right there to help you. But don't get mad at those who don't automatically anticipate your needs. After my parents died, a friend told me, "We all want to help you, but none of us knows what to do. You need to tell us what you need." So I started doing that. If there was someone who hadn't called me, I called him or her. I'd say, "Hey, I need you to go for a walk with me." Or, "Let's go to dinner." Instead of stewing about people who aren't there for you, let them know what they can do. They are probably already wondering how they can help.

8) Accept that friendship is not a quid pro quo experience. You get what you give, but not always from the people you give it to. You may have been a truly great friend to someone, but when you really need that person, he or she is nowhere to be found. This can be a source of real hurt or anger, but that's the way it goes in life. But then, you will be heartened when someone you never expected to embrace you stands up in a very big way. Focus on the people who hold you up rather than those who let you down.

9) Loud music, dancing, and art are restorative. Who knew? Maybe you stopped blasting your stereo after college, but in dark moments, singing and dancing to loud music can be quite healing. More than thirty studies found significant reductions in anxiety and depression when individuals attended art classes, listened to familiar music, or danced. Maybe it's because the people who created those pieces were trying to face life, too.

10) Go outside. Sunlight increases the amount of serotonin in your brain, creating an extremely potent and fast-acting antidepressant. It's an obvious antidote for people suffering from winter depression, but more than a dozen studies have found it to be extremely effective in helping other kinds of depression as well. A thirty-minute outdoor walk gives you a double boost — bright light *and* exercise.

11) Show up. Just show up — and keep showing up. It doesn't matter that you want to do a phenomenal job and exceed expectations every time. Sometimes you can't. When everything falls apart, sometimes the only thing you *can* do is show up.

12) Drop the ball. If you are juggling too much, drop the ball every now and again. On purpose. Just let it go. There comes a point when you must choose between imperfection and insanity. Choose imperfection every time. You simply cannot function at 100 percent all day, every day. You're no good to others if you're no good to yourself. Sometimes, you've got to drop the ball.

13) Force yourself to leave the house. How will you ever kick-start your mojo if you're curled up in a fetal position on your couch? Emotional malaise always gets worse when you surrender to a lifeless life. If you must sit in a stupor, at least go do it on a park bench or in a coffee shop or at your favorite bookstore. Leave the house, even if it's only for ten minutes.

14) Overpower catastrophic thinking. You can easily obsess that the worst possible outcome is probably going to happen — even when it's totally unrealistic. Some people feel an ache in their side and are sure it's cancer. Well, if you expect bad things to happen, bad things *will* happen. If you think you will find trouble, you *will* find trouble. Ground yourself in reality. If it isn't happening right now, how likely is it that it actually will happen? *Really*? Get into the present moment and ask yourself: 1) Am I making matters worse by thinking this way? 2) How likely is it to actually play out like that? 3) Can I change my focus? Refocus and take action to move things in a more positive direction.

15) When all else fails, do a hard reset. Sometimes things don't get better on their own. Sometimes you have to hit the big reset button. It is the grand cure-all that is a real life changer. Mine was the beach walk. This book will help you find yours.

ABOUT ASKING FOR HELP

I can't overstate this or leave it to a simple bullet point. You aren't in this alone, so don't pressure yourself into thinking that you are. Don't be so prideful that you can't ask your neighbors or friends or church members to help you out when you need it. People feel good when they can make a difference in the life of someone they care about. And sometimes it's the only way you will ever get caught up.

Everything I owned was boxed up and ready for a move into a house that I'd been renovating for months when I realized my father was about to die. I didn't know how long he had. Days? Weeks? But I knew it was getting close. I also knew I had to move before that happened. If I waited until he passed, I would not be able to face the towers of boxes. It would have been too much. I knew that as well.

So I sent an e-mail to a few of my friends that said, "I NEED HELP." On moving day, all ten of the people I'd written showed up to unpack me once everything had been moved into my new home. Collectively, they were able to do in a few hours what would have taken me months to complete in the cloud of my grief. My dad died three days later, knowing I was settled in my new home. Believe me, I knew how blessed I was to have those friends.

If you need help making things work, ask for help. And when you are needed, give help. The collective energy of our support network is one of the most affirming gifts in our lives.

COPING TAKES PRACTICE

Instead of waiting for life to get easier — which it often doesn't — find ways to make yourself stronger. Practice coping skills that will center you so you can move into a more positive state of being.

Ground yourself. Buck up. Carry on.

Within you — and around you — is the way out of your woes.

While knowing that there is always someone who has it worse than you doesn't help to fix what is wrong in your world, it does give you perspective.

It is such a gift if you wake up, are healthy, feel love (even if only from your dog), are safe, and have hope.

It is such a gift that you live in a part of the world where you can speak freely, believe what you want to believe, live where you want to live, love who you want to love, and dream what you want to dream.

There are millions of people who can't.

It is so easy to perceive life as an endless challenge, but you should also see it for its incoming tide of blessings, especially when you realize how your troubles are strengthening you.

If you have lost hope, you can find it again.

Just for a minute.

Look.

At.

Today.

It is your miracle.

CHAPTER 14

AFFIRM THYSELF

To the cynics of the world, affirmations are a big crock of woo-woo BS. But to me, a recovered cynic who believes wholeheartedly in the actual science involved, affirmations are one of the most potent cures for the challenges you face in life.

They seem so simple. But it's usually the simple things that help move us forward.

The science of affirmations, pioneered by French psychologist Emile Coué in the 1920s, works like this: Your brain is like a computer. It's like a hard drive. It works according to a program. Whatever you program into it — whatever is on that hard drive in your head — is what your brain believes.

If you program your internal hard drive with fear, doubt, and negativity, it will function in a realm of fear, doubt, and negativity. But if you program it to respond with strength, confidence, and positivity, guess what? Your brain will direct you to operate in a realm of strength, confidence, and positivity.

And science has proven that all of us have great power to do that, if we just get with the program. Your brain will believe whatever you tell it to believe — even if it is 100 percent wrong. So when you tell yourself something over and over and over, your brain will accept it and believe it — good or bad.

Write down ten negative things you have told yourself this week and really look at them. Are those things grounded in reality? Would other people say those things about you? And would they say them with such vitriol?

Don't be skeptical about the value of positive self-talk until you really look at the power and influence of all the *negative* self-talk you have put into your brain. The world is filled with thin people who think they're fat, smart people who think they're stupid, beautiful people who think they're ugly, strong people who think they're weak, and charming people who think they're awkward.

Conversely, you have also seen people who think they are really smart (but are really dolts), who think they are handsome (but are hideous), who think they are suave (but are buffoons). These people may have gotten those messages in childhood, or they may have adopted them as adults. Either way, they buy into those false messages as their truth, and that truth becomes what their brains believe is their reality.

That's the interesting thing about that internal hard drive. It never does a reality check. So let's say you are overweight. Can you program your brain to think you are thin? You can. And here's the beauty of this: if you tell yourself, "I am thin and beautiful" enough times, studies show that your brain will believe it, and you will start to lose weight.

People need that positivity in their lives. That's why inspirational posters sell like crazy and why people post nice quotes all over social media. The world has more than enough negativity, but if we can train our brains to think happy thoughts, then we gain the promise of happiness in our lives as well.

Affirmations work, but you have to work them. You have to say them. To think them. Over and over. Because when you stop repeating your affirmations, they lose their effectiveness.

You tend to believe your most strongly embedded thoughts, and if you've been negative a lot longer than you've been positive, the negativity will come creeping back. But if you keep repeating your affirmations, the positive thoughts will eventually overwrite the negative ones.

Affirmations are incredibly powerful tools for coping. You can use them to help you cope with daily difficulties, hypercharge your career, improve your self-esteem and self-image, open yourself up in your relationship, and give yourself greater focus and better balance in your life.

But there *is* a catch.

They only work when you are ready to make them work.

Over the years, I've used positive affirmations to deal with tough situations, face difficult people, and get things done.

But the moment I really thought I needed them — when my mom died — I couldn't even say them. A week after she passed away, I wrote nine affirmations, including, "Even though I am in the grief process, I feel happiness and joy" and "I am Betty Germer's daughter, and I am strong and happy."

But I just couldn't say, much less repeat, any of those

things. I wasn't ready. There was no talking myself out of grief until I'd grieved.

Then my dad died, and it got even worse.

But the day the Chicago song *Feelin' Stronger Every Day* came on the radio, I latched onto its refrain and repeated it over and over and over and over. *"Knowing that you would have wanted it this way, I do believe I'm feelin' stronger every day."* I said it to myself hundreds of times, maybe thousands.

And it started working. It was the one affirmation I believed.

I was ready.

Are you?

Here is how to create your own affirmations:

1. You must write down your affirmations. This will cement them in your mind. Simply thinking them isn't enough.

2. Start by writing five positive affirmations to deal with your specific challenge.

3. Be as general or as specific as you feel you need to be. These are just for you.

4. Always write them in the affirmative. For example, "I am free of stress and worry" is better than "I am not going to let this stress me out." "I think only positive thoughts" beats "I don't think negative thoughts anymore."

5. Now write them on Post-Its, and place them in places you look every day — your bathroom mirror, the fridge door, in your car, at your desk, in your planner, and so on.

Now that you have five ready, here's how to work your affirmations:

1. On the first two days, repeat your series of affirmations 50 times each at different times during the day.

2. Say them thirty times each for the third and fourth days.

3. Then say them twenty or twenty-five times a day for the next two weeks.

4. After that, say them three to ten times a day until you realize that they have worked because you are accepting those positive truths naturally and automatically.

5. The more you repeat them, the more you will believe them.

6. They work well when said silently, but they're even better when spoken aloud while looking into the mirror. Many people tape them to their bathroom mirrors and say them while getting ready for their day.

Here are a few examples:

1. I am strong enough to handle this and any challenge that comes my way.

2. I'm really proud of myself.

3. This is getting easier every single day.

4. I focus on the positive things in my life. I see only what is positive.

5. I am happy and alive.

6. These are great times.

7. I am so grateful for all of the wonder in my life.

8. I am strong and capable of handling anything.

The tapes inside your head are extremely powerful. If you repeat a negative remark enough times, it will load itself onto the permanent memory of your personal internal hard drive. I don't believe you have the power to completely erase those tapes because it does seem like they are ready and willing to play themselves again as soon as you stop repeating your affirmations. But you do have great control over your personal tapes, and you possess the ability to overwrite the bad ones. You can — and should — record positive, constructive, and productive affirmations. Your psyche will absorb them, use them, and — most importantly — believe them if you repeat them often enough.

Affirmations will not work for you if you don't work them. It takes only a few minutes a day, even if you are repeating your set of affirmations fifty times throughout the day.

Isn't that little bit of effort worth it for a life-changing payoff?

CHAPTER 15

RESETTING MYSELF

Everything unraveled in 2013. My mom and dad died in my arms less than three months apart. My seven-year relationship fell apart. My new home had hugely expensive issues the inspector had missed. And one of my best friends proved to be my worst.

After a year of grief and sadness, something had to give.

I make my living onstage as a motivational speaker. I teach people how to take charge of their lives. Happiness is a choice, I'd say. Thoughts are powerful, and you manifest what your mind expects, good or bad. And I believed it all because it had always worked.

Until it didn't.

Inside, I was crumbling. My heart was broken. There weren't many outward signs of what was happening to me, but it was real. I'd put on some weight. I wasn't laughing. I wasn't going out as much, and I wasn't engaging with people in my usual way.

That whole year is still a blur to me. Crisis, grief, and sadness enveloped me, and something had to give.

Somehow, I managed to function well onstage. But offstage, I was lost. I was desperate for some sort of a reset.

I saw an announcement for a fire walk on Meetup.com. Yes, you read that right. Fire walk. As in, walk over hot coals in my bare feet. The announcement promised I would "... discover the hidden potential that remains dormant ..."

I'll try that, I thought.

Talk about a cry for help.

The event turned into more of a journey than I had expected. We were told we would progress through a number of empowerment exercises that would culminate in the fire walk. Imagine my surprise when our leaders unfurled a comforter and spread about 100 pounds of broken glass in a path for us to traverse. Yes, glass. Real glass – beer bottles and the like.

"Relax," our leader told us. Walking on broken glass with scary jagged edges would feel just like walking on seashells on the beach, she said.

No way, I thought, but once I saw two people make it from one side to the other, I realized it was possible, and I was in. *I can do that*, I thought.

So I did.

I'm a little embarrassed sharing that. What kind of sane person would need — or want — to walk over broken glass? Yet I did it.

I share this because it's crucial in order to understand why a reset is sometimes imperative. My normally good coping skills were failing me. They weren't working. I was absolutely desperate for a jolt of new energy, something that worked in the way a defibrillator restarts the heart.

But it turned out that walking over broken glass was not the answer. Just a sad symptom of my melancholy.

I hoped the upcoming fire walk would be my cure. A metaphor for going through something difficult and then coming out okay on the other side. But really, it wouldn't be that hard. I'd done my research and learned that it's not dangerous to walk over hot coals. The ash insulates your feet. The risk is minimal.

Once the coals were hot and ready, we were told how to walk in a circle, chanting, then cross over the coals in the middle of the circle when we were ready.

But things went very wrong. A man tripped, and the woman behind him fell as well. They disrupted the ash. And our leader seemed much more worried about calming the energy in the air than about the coals under our feet. I was the next person to walk through the fire, and I felt the hot coals burn my feet. Every single one of us burned our feet that night.

Our leader told us to put our feet in the dirt and "let Mother Earth" heal us. I did that, but the longer we were there, the more my feet hurt.

I mean, *hurt.*

Mother Earth was not helping.

We finally got out of there after midnight. I will always treasure the memory of me limping in pain with my dirt-covered, burned feet through the 24-hour Super Walmart as I searched for aloe, cursing the whole nutty notion I'd had that such foolishness would reset my life.

By the time I got home, my feet were blistered and throbbing. It was evidence of what a huge miscalculation I'd made, trying this seemingly fun way to give myself a jolt.

When I woke up a few hours later, the weirdest thing happened. My feet were fine. No blisters, no scars, no redness, nothing. It was like nothing had happened the night before.

I was no worse for wear.

But I was also no better, either.

HITTING BOTTOM

It was pretty clear I was desperate for something, and looking back on that time, I see that the weeks preceding my reset were filled with an almost frantic search for some miracle cure.

Right after the January 4 anniversary of my mom's death, I jetted off for Dallas, where I would keynote for Deloitte at its 800-bed hotel and state-of-the-art meeting center. Sadly, it was the same hotel where I'd keynoted a year earlier — the day after my mom died. There I was, a year later, in the same place with the same people, my heart and soul in an even darker place because I now knew the crippling dimensions of grief.

It was my darkest moment. I was lost — truly lost.

Hot coals weren't enough. Nothing was enough. I had hit my emotional rock bottom.

I contemplated getting antidepressants, but it was there in Dallas, in my deepest moments of despair, that it hit me.

I suddenly knew exactly what I had to do.

I'd pull a Forrest Gump. On the beach.

I would put myself back together.

I made the decision at 2 a.m. that Sunday morning, and I came up with a plan. I flew home that afternoon, and I started walking the next day. I was ready for my reset.

It was the most significant thing I have ever done in my life. It was my greatest gift to myself.

THE WALK

On Monday, I woke up, cleared my schedule, and headed to Fort De Soto. My only prep was looking at Google Earth and calculating some distances with Map My Walk. I guessed it would take me eight or nine days to go from end to end, longer once I found my way by boat to the barrier islands. Some beaches would be busy with people, others empty. I didn't know what the weather would do. But none of that mattered.

Armed with sunscreen, a hat, two GPS apps, and one fragile psyche, I locked my bike at one end of Fort De Soto Park, a pristine Gulf island in St. Petersburg, Florida, then drove my car to the other end.

I was ready to walk.

I would walk Pinellas County's Gulf coastline — more than 70 miles —even the parts so remote I could only access them by kayak, ferry, or motorboat. Spending endless hours walking where the water meets the sky would heal my hurt. I knew it.

This was my Forrest Gump moment. When Forrest had had enough of life's rigors, he started running across the country. I had no plan for how far I would walk each day or how long it would take. All I knew was that I was done being sad. Every day, I would drop my bike, move the car, and then walk back to where I'd left my bike. After cycling back to the car, I'd drive home, sleep in my own bed, then drive right back the next morning to where I'd left off the day before.

The previous year, I had probably walked 400 miles

on north Clearwater Beach, Caladesi Island, and north Honeymoon Island. We have endless miles of coastline in my county, but like just about everybody else, I always picked my closest beach and walked the same stretch over and over.

And that's such a profound metaphor for how most of us live our lives. Familiarity is comfortable, but our real growth happens out there where we *haven't* walked.

Easy to say, harder to learn.

That first day was 72 degrees with deep blue skies. When I set off, the first thing I saw was the Skyway Bridge in the distance. I stood on the sand of the ten-mile tropical island, thinking how I'd crossed that bridge every week for the last fifteen years to visit my mom and dad. A pang of grief shot through me, but it didn't last as I thought about what I'd survived.

On my second day, it rained all morning. I debated whether to even walk. The clouds over Pass-a-Grille hung low and ready to open up. Other people saw a blah day and found something else to do, but I started to groove on the drama in the sky. They weren't thunderclouds. The worst thing that could happen was that I'd get wet. Another metaphor for life. Just push through the hard stuff, because it may not be as bad as it looks.

It didn't rain. I realized that all of my senses were hyper-performing as I walked. I was so present. Not depressed, but not really happy, either. Just very, very aware of what I was seeing and feeling.

I slept straight through the night, something I hadn't done in a while. I woke up excited, almost giddy. For the first time in a very long time, I was more interested in what was in front of me than what was behind me.

I walked alone, and at first, I told very few people about it and did not post online. I wasn't walking to get attention. I did text pictures to my former partner, Julie, and I called her at the end of each day to tell her what I'd done. Something was shifting in my mind about us, but I didn't force myself to figure it out. I could tell I was opening back up.

On I walked. I became intoxicated by wide-open space, blue sky, and big waters. I embraced everything I saw. There was a dad beaming as his little girl showed off her cartwheels in Treasure Island. On Indian Rocks Beach, I shared a belly laugh with a guy who had struggled incredibly hard to reel in the tiniest fish in the whole Gulf of Mexico. I saw a young couple making out in a lifeguard stand on Sand Key and warmed at the memory of doing that myself on a beach a million years ago.

I walked Pinellas' contiguous coastline for eight consecutive days, then covered four keys on four more days in the next two weeks. To get to those remote islands, I had to either paddle my kayak, take a ferry, or get a boat ride out. Throughout the adventure, I had short and long days, ranging from three miles to thirteen and a half.

Along the way, I saw impressive cloud formations, treacherous waves, pods of dolphins, an inexcusable amount of trash at Fort De Soto and Shell Key, dogs frolicking on dog beaches, palm trees, driftwood, seashells, sand dollars, a dead bonnethead shark, and three guys wearing see-through thongs.

It was as if I were walking straight into my soul.

Things that shouldn't matter didn't matter. And I didn't have time to feel sad — I was too busy welling up with wonder and gratitude.

My hardest day was a 39- to 43-degree, windy, 9.9-mile haul from Redington Beach to north Belleair Beach. The wind came straight at my face at times, and under normal circumstances one would either seek shelter or give up. But it was in those relentlessly windy moments that I achieved my greatest clarity because all I could do was take the next step. And the next.

I have told this to so many thousands of people onstage: You don't know how close you are to turning the corner until you turn the corner. That cold wind tried to push me back, but I kept moving forward.

At some point, I noticed I was talking to myself, out loud. "Thank you, thank you, thank you," I was saying. On the fourth day, when I saw the pink Hyatt Regency ahead on the distant Clearwater Beach, I heard myself say, "There's Clearwater. There's Clearwater! I'm home." There was so much prayer, and all of it was gratitude.

The final part of my quest was the islands accessible only by boat: Egmont Key, Shell Key, Three Rooker Bar, and Anclote Key. They are, by far, the most exquisite pieces of nature I have experienced in Florida. And for the first time, I wasn't walking alone. My friend hiked Three Rooker Bar with me after she and her husband ferried me out there. We stood, mouths agape, as smiling baby dolphins jumped like Flipper and raced on top of the waves.

The last day, on Anclote Key, Julie and some of my best friends were anchored on a pontoon boat offshore, watching me make it to the end. The end of that island was the end of my quest. And they cheered when I got there.

I needed to do something to mark the finish line, so I got on my knees to write in the sand. I didn't want to overthink it.

"DONE," I wrote.

Looking back, it was the right word. Sure, I was done walking. But I was also done feeling like a victim.

I was done with the darkness. I'd turned the corner.

CHAPTER 16

HOW TO DO A HARD RESET

So you've come to the realization that it's time to reset. Maybe you're a little apprehensive. You're asking, now what? How do resets work?

Most stories are so neatly told: beginning, middle, end.

But life does not always unfold all that neatly, and when a reset is involved, you go a little backwards: first you must mark an ending, then a middle, and then a new beginning. Finish what was, let go and work through it, then emerge with a new beginning.

The actual reset is the point in the middle where you deliberately end the old and begin anew.

That new beginning is your ultimate goal. Always remember that as you set out on your own reset journey.

WHAT KIND OF RESET WILL WORK FOR YOU?

There is no cookie-cutter reset. I spent many, many hours hiking my local beaches. That might work for you. Or maybe something else is calling to you. A reset is your gift to yourself. It is you prioritizing yourself and taking charge of your emotional health. Do it your way. Make it your own.

The main elements of a good reset are:

1. Make time. How long will your reset take? Well, how long do you have? How much time can you invest in taking your life back? If your time is limited, be creative. Figure out something extraordinary you can do with twenty-four or forty-eight hours. If you have more time to spend, find a journey or quest that will allow you to dig deep and do the processing you need to do.

2. Make it grand so you will notice. What will change if you do something you've always done? Nothing. Be bold. Doing something new gives you a reason to wake up energized in the morning. It gives you something to look forward to.

3. Create a challenge. When you achieve something that you never imagined achieving, you feel strong, able, and viable. Why not insert an element of challenge into your reset so you know you have accomplished something significant?

4. Change your pace. Slow down. Or speed up. It may help to noticeably change gears in order to shake up your body's rhythm and wake up your inner self. Some people reset by slowing down so they can hear themselves think, but others need to speed it up a little in order to wake up.

5. Enjoy some solitude. You may benefit from quiet time. A lot of it. Imagine the luxury of time to pray or to venture deep into your head. Conversely, you may be re-energized when you are around people. On some level, you know whether you need to do this alone or with others. Just remember that this is all about you. It's about you processing the experience so you can recharge and move forward.

6. Get physical. It is a fact that exercise can be the

fastest and most potent intervention for the blues. Exercise boosts your endorphins — the "feel good" hormones. Extended exercise alone can be enough to give you the jolt you need. But if you combine it with some of the other reset factors, you will really be energized.

7. Go outdoors. Whether or not you are a great outdoorsperson, go outside and breathe in some fresh air. When you expose your skin to the sun, you get the natural Vitamin D that has been proven to help with depression. It will naturally elevate your mood. Plus, soaking in some sunshine as you sled downhill on short, cold winter days can absolutely be curative.

My reset has changed my life. I needed a reset because I was in a depressive loop. If I didn't do something, my life would continue exactly as it was. I was done with that. I was ready to do something.

Are you?

When I was figuring out my reset, I knew I needed a huge amount of time exercising alone in vast open space with no music and no interruptions.

And I needed a definable challenge. Instead of deciding to go for a few long beach walks, I threw in the added challenge of walking the full length of my county's beaches, plus the barrier islands. I'd never heard of anyone doing anything like that, most likely because the insufferable traffic in Pinellas County meant the starting points of my first four walks were as much as an hour and fifteen minutes away. Some walks required me to go out and back to where I started because I was hiking an island or a remote peninsula. The mere logistics of my reset made the goal something extraordinary. My walk checked off every element on my list.

It gave me the time I needed to do something substantial. It was all new to me. It was a challenge that progressed slowly enough for me to process the things I needed to process. And I did it alone, with no interruptions.

MENTAL HEALTH

I made the choice to reset instead of doing therapy or taking antidepressants, but I feel certain that a reset would also work well in unison with those treatments. It can't hurt. It can only help. And if you think you need more, why not use every resource available to you?

We live in a time where people do not need to hide the fact that they have experienced depression, used antidepressants, or sought psychological help. That shame existed in another century. Right now, one in ten Americans are on antidepressants, and one in four women between the ages of forty and sixty are using them — that, according to researchers at the Johns Hopkins Bloomberg School of Public Health.

There are no rules for your own personal reset. You come up with your own formula. But if you are still needing guidance, here are some suggestions.

THE STEPS

Reset is a process.

Decide to put yourself first. Depending on the obligations in your personal life, this may or may not be an issue. A single parent is going to have more of a challenge clearing a schedule, but it's imperative to do so if the alternative is a breakdown or complete life dysfunction. There has to be a way. Life is too short to be so out of control of your time that you can't make enough space to take care of yourself in a moment of inner crisis. Find out what you can do, and then do it.

Brainstorm your magic cure. Don't let some author or speaker or coach or talk show host tell you what will work for you. Only you know what turns you on. Find something you love — something you truly love. Or something that makes you go deep. Or something that centers you. What really matters is that your soul's cure is something you know means something to you on a profound level.

Visualize the end result. We often fall into funks because we don't have anything to look forward to. Goals change that. Challenges are, in themselves, rewards. They change the norm. They shake up our routine.

Give yourself enough time. Be realistic about how much time you will need to achieve your reset. Don't underestimate it. There is something invigorating about devoting time to yourself. Not just fifteen minutes, not just a day, but as much time as you need. So *take* that time. Don't delay because you can't get an entire month off, but don't rush any more than you have to. Reclaiming your life is more important than the other things on your to-do list because your to-do list will be so much easier to handle once you have reclaimed your life.

Scope it out. Do the research. Figure out what it will take to pull it off. What are the logistics, the finances?

What's the best timing? What kind of support will you need?

Just do it. Don't make it more difficult than it needs to be. The more you plan and overthink, the more difficult it becomes. If it is too complex, you may cheat yourself out of the magic of a stress-free reset. Granted, if you're going to climb to Base Camp on Mount Everest, you're going to have to do a great deal of planning. And a big part of that reset likely occurs in the planning process because anticipation can be curative. But there comes a point when you have to stop planning and start doing.

Commit. "I'm going to ..." is useless without commitment. Commit to your reset. You are not doing it "sooner or later" or "one of these days." You are *doing* it. It might not be tomorrow, but you *are* going to do it. You must actively commit, plan, check off your action steps, and move forward. Check your calendar, figure out your timing, pick your date, and commit. I'd actually planned to do a pilgrimage-type beach walk for four days that would take me up part of Florida's East Coast to finish on New Year's in St. Augustine. Do you know why I didn't do it? It looked like it might rain — which it didn't. And what if it had? If you are going to do it, DO IT.

Start. You don't have to have every single detail figured out and accounted for. Over-planning can be an excuse for delay. And delay is the first step to backing out. If you are going to do something drastic, do it. Dive in. Get moving. What you are doing right now isn't working, so wake up, get yourself together, and go.

Let go. Whatever happens is probably going to be very different from what you expect. Embrace the moment for whatever it holds. Find your rhythm, enjoy being present. This is a gift to yourself, so let go of whatever it was that was holding you down and repeat this mantra: "I am open and ready for all good things." As you move through your reset, let go of the old and embrace the new.

Breathe in the moment. Your reset is a gift to yourself, one you should savor. Don't rush it, don't think ahead, don't look back. Be right where you are, cherishing the gift for all it can and should stand for. It is a huge deal to take hold of your power and use it to leave the darkness and enter the light. Fill the experience with hope and possibility. If you feel yourself being dragged back into what you are leaving behind, consciously let go. Say, "I'm here now. This is fresh, it's new. I see only hope and possibility." Drink in the moment because it marks a new beginning, and the moment will come when you realize what a gift it was.

Commemorate the experience. Journal, take pictures — whatever works for you. Make a picture book or frame something. Have a symbol to remind you that you took your power, you turned the page, and you made the change.

Write down memory prompts. At some point, what you learned from your experience will become evident to you. Write down every lesson, every insight, every positive emotion so that you will have it to come back to in order to continue your growth.

Your growth doesn't have to stop because you return to familiar surroundings. Your restart gave you a jolt, a kick start, a new beginning. But if you don't deliberately review and renew, you will lose your progress and slide back into the place you once were. Whether you continue growing depends on whether you continue to reinforce your lessons and move toward the light of your new day.

It may be difficult for the new, improved you to go back to familiar surroundings that may have been previously dark, but it doesn't mean that you have to slide back to where you were when you began your reset. It's up to you to remember what you learned.

Plan the next step. You have a powerful new coping tool, so use it. You may have taken a week for self-discovery, but plan for an exciting day for a booster shot. If you see a potential moment of difficulty ahead, make a plan for a mini-reset. Find a way to go back to that space, even if it's only with photographs, because healing needs to be reinforced so that growth can continue.

Believe. It can be intimidating to take your power and hold the responsibility for your emotional well-being. You may wonder what will happen if your reset doesn't work. Well, it won't work if you don't believe in it. It may not give you what you expect. Maybe it won't fix everything. Maybe it will fix more than you ever imagined. But believe in it. Be open to it. Let it work for you. A lot of depression is fueled by negativity, so you have to consciously put that at bay so that you can be open to a full reset. If you don't think it will work, guess what? It probably won't. Isn't that how life goes?

RIGHT, BUT HOW LONG WILL IT LAST?

The cynical side of me expected the darkness to return shortly after the beach walk ended. Surely the depression was just waiting in the shadows to swallow me up again.

It didn't.

All I needed to do was look at the pictures of my

walk, and I'd go back to the exhilaration I'd felt in that open space. I had a great new tool. I just needed to continue doing long beach walks so I'd feel that rush again.

I made the decision to hit the reset button when I didn't know what else to do. I don't have to wait that long anymore. I now know what works for me, and when I see trouble coming, I will make a plan to help myself by taking a very long beach walk.

By the time the first anniversary of my dad's death came around, I'd already done my walk.

Instead of fearing the anniversary, I made a plan. I would get up early, drive down to Manatee County and walk the ten-mile length of Anna Maria Island.

Manatee is the next county south from me. It's where my parents lived and where I lived for high school and part of college. The Gulf waters are even more spectacular than ours here in Pinellas. So the idea of doing an all-day walk on that beach called

"This is the beginning of anything you want."

— *Unknown*

"Sometimes the smallest step in the right direction ends up being the biggest step of your life. Tiptoe if you must, but take the step."

— *Anonymous*

"There was nowhere to go but everywhere, so just keep rolling under the stars."

— *Jack Kerouac*

to me. I looked forward to that day, knowing my time there would give me the space I needed for prayer and remembrance.

I started walking at 9:20 a.m. at the Anna Maria City Pier. I remembered a restaurant there that my family used to always go to. And then I walked past the old Rod and Reel Pier. I used to fish off that pier in college, and Mom and Dad would visit me when I was out there with my dog. And then there was the park where I'd had a recent Father's Day picnic with my dad. And the swing set where my mom and I swung back and forth when we were both adults. Every turn gave me a memory of growing up with the best parents I could have ever asked for.

But instead of drowning in grief and loss, I was alive with gratitude and joy. There were so many happy memories, and they came back to me with intensity. I was so blessed to be out there that beautiful day, and I was happy. Deeply happy. Overjoyed.

It was one of the best days of my life.

I had the secret of what would work for me: a mini-reset. Time in the fresh air, one foot in front of the other.

The sand on Anna Maria was softer than on my beaches, making it more challenging for me. It was exhausting, but I knew that all I had to do was keep putting one foot in front of the other. I would get there.

I would get there.

CHAPTER 17

GROWING YOUR RESILIENCE

Years ago, I became friends with a lawyer who was awesome beyond words. She operated out of pure integrity, and she was generous, kind, and deep. She had everything going on.

It was amazing, especially since she'd come out of a home where her schizophrenic mother had been physically and emotionally abusive and her father had never been there.

Considering how well she turned out, it was interesting to think that her sister was a nasty, lonely, miserable person who could barely function in this world.

How did these two people come out of the same horrible situation with completely different outcomes?

The answer is *resilience*.

Is resilience something we're born with or something we develop?

Some people just are resilient. Others make a conscious choice to live that way.

So many people chase the dream of the perfect marriage, happy family, beautiful home, prosperous career — a life where the sun shines all the time.

Then reality slaps them in the face.

The marriage falls apart.

Or somebody gets sick.

Maybe the job ends abruptly.

Or the house winds up in foreclosure.

Somebody is a victim of a crime.

A natural disaster strikes.

All you have to do is live a while to realize that life never unfolds according to plan and your happiness depends on your ability to cope with and adapt to an ever-changing reality.

If you weren't born strong, you can still *be* strong.By this point in my life, I've watched enough weak people and mighty people deal with life, and it's clear that we often can't control what happens to us, but we can always control how we process and deal with it. Weak people don't say, "I like being weak! I like making weak decisions! I like being a victim!" They just slide into that mode because they fail to make the decision to take the power that's available to them — the power that every one of us can have. They simply fail to live powerfully.

DIG DEEP, LIVE BOLD

I have been so inspired by a woman who was brought to this country by a husband who isolated, tortured, and beat her for years. He monitored her every move. He followed her. When he started to abuse their daughter, she found a way to break free, moving with her little girl to a battered women's shelter. When we first met, she spoke in very broken English and had no education and no resources.

That was three years ago. Lyn is a completely different woman now.

She made up her mind to prevail. She was done being a victim.

No more, no more, no more, *no more!*

I met her shortly after she and her daughter moved away from the main shelter into a transitional housing program where I volunteer. This program gave her a two-bedroom apartment behind a protective ten-foot gate, rent-free for two years.

Lyn was so very, very determined to make it.

Every day, she'd ride her bicycle for miles to get to work, even in the worst Florida heat. It was raining so hard one day that she had no choice but to call a taxi because she would never skip work or be late. That cab driver deliberately drove an incorrect and out-of-the-way route, charging her more money than she made that whole day.

But the next day, Lyn got up, ready for a new day. I never once saw her feel sorry for herself.

One day, she could not wait to tell me her news. She had gotten her driver's license and had immediately gone to get a brand new car. Long ago, she'd made up her mind to save for the day when she passed that test and could get transportation. This was huge news because no one else in the transitional housing complex had managed such a feat. She was so proud!

Two weeks later, she was in a wreck. But she got up the day after it happened, got the car to the body shop, and got on about her business. She was smiling again.

She'd been such a model client that the center was going to extend her stay in her apartment for another year — at no charge. But Lyn didn't want the extension.

She'd socked away enough money to leave the program and live on her own.

I have no doubt about her making it in this world because she has everything she needs to face what life will throw at her. She has resolve, and she has resolved to be resilient.

Whenever I start to feel frustrated, I think about Lyn riding her bicycle on those busy, hot roads. She always, always had hope. And she always had her goals and dreams. Inside, she always knew she would find a way.

Obviously, she did not always have that inner power because of the situation she originally found herself in. But once she had her freedom, she made a conscious decision to dig deep and live bold.

We all have that power.

I look at others in the same transitional housing and see some who have chosen resolve and some who are still too weak to find it. The ones who struggle most often use the words "I can't." The ones who I watch grow more powerful every month are the ones who say, "I will find a way."

One of the women made me so sad because her mother had been diagnosed with Stage IV liver and lung cancer, but this woman was too afraid of her mother dying to bring herself to visit, even though her mom was just fifteen minutes away.

"I don't know how to be strong!" she cried.

"Start by making one strong decision," I told her. "Just go for an hour."

If you don't know how you are going to take your power and reset, start small. One strong decision, then another strong decision, and then another. Do it one at a time and after a while, you will get so used to making strong decisions, they'll come to you naturally.

"But I can't!" she answered.

"Oh yes you can," I told her. "And whenever you think you can't, I want you to think of Lyn riding her bike in that heat. She made up her mind to do it. That's all you have to do."

Make up your mind. Be done with being the victim.

GET OUTTA VICTIMHOOD

Coming from the newspaper industry (which has lost more than 55,000 newsroom jobs in recent years), I have seen truly competent people face professional collapse. As I watch how my old colleagues have landed, I have seen something rather incredible. Whether they succeeded or struggled had little to do with talent and everything to do with resolve.

If you can't get it together, you are stuck in your victimhood. Agility and resilience will lift you out of your difficulties, but you have to choose to dig down and use the courage that you absolutely have within you.

It is harder and more exhausting to choose to be weak and live as a victim than it is to choose to be strong. Every single time I have taken the easy way out, it wound up being way harder than if I'd just done things the hard way in the first place.

Clinical depression is the wild card that can trump all of the self-help work you do. That biological issue makes it hard to find inner strength. If you are fighting to get out of bed in the morning, there is no way you can read a chapter in a book, follow six little steps, and be completely cured. You have to deal with the depression first. It's your body. Clinical depression is a physiological issue. Don't blame yourself for it.

A lot of depression is situational, and self-care can lift you out of it. That means eating, sleeping, and exercising right, and leaning on your support network. You create your resilience, and your resilience moves you into the light.

The Japanese proverb, "Fall down seven times, get up eight" is what I live by. Life will throw a lot at you, and there will always be times when it will seem impossible to realize or access your power. But just remember it's there. You really do have all the power you need. If you know you will always get up — no matter what — you will never be diminished by adversity.

Here is how to move through your difficulties with a powerful, resilient spirit:

Feel what you feel. You can't tell yourself that everything is fabulous when it really sucks. What you can do is look at your feelings, acknowledge them, then consciously come up with a way to move forward.

Make up your mind. If being a victim is not working for you, stop being a victim. If making weak choices is not serving you well, choose to change. Be strong. You do have it in you.

Be grateful. I've said it so many times already. Gratitude is the antidote for so many of our difficulties. Instead of wallowing in what's wrong, lift yourself up by remembering what is right.

Believe in yourself. And if you don't believe in yourself, use affirmations to grow your self-confidence and self-esteem. Say, "I'm strong enough to get through this." "I believe in myself." "I cannot be stopped."

Expect obstacles. Don't judge yourself by what you accomplish that comes easily. Judge yourself by what you do when things get hard.

Shed your denial. Denial creates great victims. You have to acknowledge a problem exists in order to overcome it.

Don't make yourself weak with worry. Remember what His Holiness the Dalai Lama said: "If it can be solved, there's no need to worry. And if it can't be solved, worry is of no use."

Stop whining. Whatever it is you are facing, someone else has it worse. Way worse. And the self-loathing and self-pitying going on in your head is doing nothing to help you. Just tell yourself, "I am strong and getting stronger every day."

Have purpose. When you know what you are fighting for, it's easier to keep fighting.

Write down your goals. It's easier to climb out of your difficulties if you have a plan. Slow down and figure out what it will take to get where you need to go. Break it all down into little baby steps that you can check off, one at a time.

Embrace change. It's inevitable. What serves you better, resisting or adapting? Learn to adapt quickly so you can identify growth opportunities.

Let go of anger. The Buddha said, "Holding on to anger is like grasping a hot coal with the intent of throwing it at someone else; you are the one who gets burned." Believe me, I know all about getting burned by hot coals.

Count on your support group. If you don't have enough friends and family to give you the support you need, start actively cultivating new friends so you can get the love, support, and input you need to deal with things. Your friends and family will get you where you need to go.

Think of what Nelson Mandela said: "The greatest glory in living lies not in never falling, but in rising every time we fall."

Or what the Amazing Elizabeth Edwards wrote: "Resilience is accepting your new reality, even if it's less good than the one you had before. You can fight it, you can do nothing but scream about what you've lost, or you can accept that and try to put together something that's good."

Face life.

CHAPTER 18

THE BODY RESET

Picture this: I am introduced to the audience, everyone is clapping, and I hobble up to the stage — on crutches. When I finally get up there, I have to *sit* to deliver my keynote.

It was awful.

Someone had suggested I tell a really great tale about what had happened to me, so I did. "I have an amazing story about how this happened, and here it is. I lived a great life. A *really* great life. I skied and danced and ran and had so much fun that my knees wore out. That's it."

It sounded good, but really, I was in pain. I already knew I needed to reset my mind and soul, but what I also needed was a reset of my body.

It was the same day that my cousin, Sharon Himelhoch, suggested something that sounded like lunacy. Sharon is a chiropractor who is trained in nutrition response.

"Before you do anything, I think you should do a five-day water fast," she said.

Seriously?

Fawn Germer go without food for five days, living only on water?

Well, I figured if I was writing a book on resetting, I

would have to include a chapter on resetting the body. I started researching water fasts, and they sounded like miracle treatments to most of the people who had reported on them. So why not? If I couldn't get through it, I'd just eat.

I did tell my doctor I wasn't going to eat for five days. While she didn't encourage the fast, she did not try to talk me out of it. If you try it, please tell your doctor. I'm not endorsing anything without medical supervision.

In the end, that fast — and a subsequent metabolic detox — were life changers for me. It was hard, and there were moments when I worried I'd done damage to my body. There are a multitude of other kinds of body detoxes that do not push you as hard as a water fast, and I suggest you consider them first.

But I do suggest you consider some sort of detox to rid your body of all the poison in your system. Our foods are filled with chemicals and hormones that make us sick. When we give our body a chance to recover and break our addictions to sugar, salt, and all the mess in our processed foods, we get a fresh start that feels so good, I can't even begin to describe it.

If you are resetting, giving yourself the jolt you need for a true fresh start, don't forget your body. It is your most sacred space. It's all yours to care for, protect, and refresh.

Sharon's suggestion that I do the water fast came on a Saturday. I started on Monday. I had a short window with no travel, and I loaded up on spring water so I could get started. The only bonus food I could have was lemon for my water.

I'd wanted to do a body detox for years. Documentaries like *Fat, Sick and Nearly Dead; Fed Up; Supersize Me; Food Inc.;* and others made me want to do something, but a lack of willpower and a clear inability to go vegan kept me eating as I'd always eaten.

How odd it was that my bad knees led me to the moment of detox. I didn't expect it. Now that I'm on the other side of this detox, it feels like every cell in my body is ecstatic. I cannot exaggerate how good I feel.

I know that people who do body detoxes and cleanses sometimes sound like food evangelists. I'm no preacher. I just want to share that I know the power of this change because now, when I detour and eat something with chemicals, I feel horrible.

So here's the story.

MY BODY RESET

Before I started fasting and just drinking water each day, I made some notes that really helped me make peace with the regimen. You've probably noticed that I'm very big on affirmations, but I'm also big on perspective. I knew that I could get through this if I remembered:

1.   I was in the desert at Burning Man for five days and I got through that.

2.   I've eaten my whole life. I've had plenty of food, and I will have plenty more in my future.

3.   Whenever I feel a hunger pang, I tell myself, "Suck it up, this isn't that long. The time will pass quickly."

4.   I know I can lick the first two days, no problem. Once I do that, it should be even easier.

5.   I am not going to be a wimp about it or make it a bigger deal than I need to. I will just remind myself that I am going to eat later.

6.   When I finish this, I will have the knowledge that I don't have to fear running out of food.

7.   If, biologically, I don't have to eat, then I DON'T HAVE TO EAT. It's all in my head.

8.   When I feel hungry, I change the subject in my head. I go do something else. I schedule something to keep busy.

9.   When I think of something I want to eat, I just tell myself, "I'll eat that next week."

Day One wasn't that bad. I had all kinds of hunger prompts, but it was clear I was hungry out of habit, not out of hunger. It's interesting how meals define our days and break things up into comfortable time segments. Without meals, there was a real monotony, and without flavor, there was a boredom I had never before experienced. I had to find distractions so I could tune out the prompts.

Day Two, *I was hungry. REALLY hungry.* And I got a headache. I was surprised by a surge of resolve that welled up within me. I felt strong taking control over food in an effort to seize power over my health. I sensed a healthier person coming out the other side of it, and that was invigorating. Inside my body, things were getting a little difficult. My stomach started growling — then roaring. It wanted food. I kept reminding myself, *I'll eat in a few days. Stop being a baby.* As soon as I'd put a hunger pang away, I'd experience another. By evening, I was dying to get something inside my belly.

Day Three, I had learned the routine: Wake up ebullient, then progress through the day until I was miserable, angry, weak, and unfocused. I definitely wasn't getting any work done. I had no brain energy, and that worried me because I had to fake it during a really important conference call. I realized that the problem time for me lasted from 2 p.m. until 7:30 p.m. Once I survived the dinner hour, I knew I was good for another day. Day Three was so much easier than Day Two, but I did obsess about what I would eat when it was all over. When I would slow down and think about what my body was *really* feeling, I realized I was not all that hungry. At least, not as hungry as you'd expect for someone who had not eaten in three days.

Day Four. Definitely not a good day. I was weak. I took my cane and tried to walk my dog around the block, but I started to faint just two houses down the street. I dropped to the ground and lay there for a few minutes before slowly heading home. Also, I turned into a bear. Grouchy! But all of my reading told me that Day Four was the day the detox would kick in. Even though I felt uncomfortable, fuzzy, lame, and mad, there was one thing I did not feel — hungry. Not in the slightest. I knew my body needed fuel, but I was so close to finishing. I made it through the day and even made it through going out to dinner in a favorite restaurant with a bunch of my friends. It had been set up before I'd started fasting, and I figured, if it was intolerable, I'd just go home. My problem was not with food on Day Four. I was just sick of feeling so weak.

I wrote in my journal: "Until I see how I feel afterwards, I won't know if it was worth it. I can't get anything done. It's not a good way to spend five days of my life, although it did give me a lot of time to examine the role of food in my life, a role that has been way too big. Food doesn't have to control me, yet it has controlled me my entire life."

Day Five. I wrote: "I am so glad this is the last day. Seriously. This is my limit, I am sure. I now have a headache and ringing in my ears. I am faint, and a muscle has seized up in my left leg. But I've made it to the fifth day.

"The minutes were excruciating, but the week flew by. I am down ten pounds from where I started and will be mad when it naturally starts coming back. The hunger has been gone since day two ..." I was fantasizing about eating gazpacho, watermelon, and chicken. "I can practically taste the food," I wrote.

Day Six, I ate. That watermelon was the best watermelon I'd ever eaten in my life. My taste buds were so alive! I was so very happy I'd done it. I started thinking about doing two-day fasts every now and again, just to retain that control over food.

But that day and for three more, I felt terrible. I mean, *awful.* I did not realize that the real detox would occur after I started eating again, but that's how it played out. I felt sick — completely devoid of energy. I wondered if I'd done something to knock my thyroid out of whack. I hadn't taken my medication while I was fasting.

But after five debilitating days of weakness post-fast, the day came when I woke up feeling great. Greater than great. Better than I had ever felt. *EVER.* I felt unstoppable.

It was a huge lesson for my own personal growth. I

became so aware of how food controls me. It has nothing to do with needing to eat. It doesn't even have much to do with *wanting* to eat. My food cravings are all about eating because eating is what I do, or what we do. That's powerful knowledge.

DETOX, PART II

Sixteen days later, I went one step further. My friend Teresa Cope, a nurse practitioner, said "If you are really going to detox, you need to do more than just stop eating. You need to do a liver detox." She ordered the stuff, and soon I was on a ten-day metabolic detox program that involved massive consumption of special shakes that were gross-looking and not delicious in any way. In fact, I kinda missed just drinking water. But on this second detox program, I was to remove certain items from my diet until I ate only cruciferous vegetables, legumes, fish, apples, and pears. I was never hungry, but I was pretty grouchy.

Finally, that detox was over, too. It wasn't hard like the first one, but it definitely made me feel like I was doing my body a huge favor.

The one-two punch of the water fast plus the metabolic detox was like a secret elixir. I was working harder and faster, I was so much more focused. I felt fantastic. I didn't crave sugar, salt, or processed foods.

The body reset was phenomenal. I cannot overstate how good it made me feel. I'm not sure it did anything to help my knees. I still wound up needing a total knee replacement. But I know that cleaning up on the inside made me stronger for the recovery.

I did not share these stories so I can come off

sounding like a sanctimonious food evangelist who has seen the light. Even though the reset killed the cravings, there have been slips. The holidays were quite a challenge. When I slipped, I felt miserable. But at least I knew what I had to do to feel like a brand-new person.

A body reset.

CHAPTER 19

RESETTING YOUR NEEDS

Jayne Bray suffered for years as the workaholic senior accountant for a local college. She was not allowed to have a social life or any semblance of sanity. You could tell how awful her job was simply by looking at her. She chain-smoked, and she was having heart trouble. She was constantly sick.

But at age fifty-nine, she went into work and quit.

Just like that.

Her plan was to sell everything and drive her van off into the sunset, bound for California, where she'd be near her daughter and grandchildren. She hired an estate sale company to get rid of her stuff — all of it — except for what she could fit in her van. Everything was priced and readied for sale. Her furniture, books, old three-ring binders — even the forks. Everything.

For all of her adult life, she'd practically killed herself to support a home that would contain her "stuff." Yet when it sold, she realized how crazy that had been.

She got $1,100 for all of her stuff. A lifetime of accumulation, and it was worth less than a mortgage payment. Unbelievable.

But at last, she was free. Sort of.

"I moved shortly after the bottom dropped out of the

economy, so when I got to California and couldn't even get a job interview, I was stunned," she said. "Since I had changed states, I wasn't eligible for unemployment. I had no income at all ...

"With the help of dear, dear friends and my new-found church, I was able to squeak by. And I do mean squeak. I filed for early retirement from the Florida Retirement System and took a big cut by filing at sixty-two instead of sixty-five. But at least I had a small income, so I was grateful."

Instead of sinking into a depression over her professional woes, she dove into volunteerism with a passion that filled her with life — *real* life. She never regained the "security" she'd had from her unhealthy old job, but she has always gotten by financially. And emotionally? She was miserable before. But that changed when she walked out the door.

Now, her soul is full and alive. At first, she worked with the homeless and the mentally ill, but for the last few years she has really been grooving on working with at-risk youths in Watts. She has more purpose than she ever did.

"With the volunteer work, I was helping someone else. I wasn't 'suffering,'" she said. "Your own suffering is always minimized when you see someone else in a worse situation than you."

When she left her job at the college, she was replaced. But what she does now? She is irreplaceable.

"I have never missed a single thing that I left behind," she said. "The 'treasures' are still with me — notes from my Great-Aunt Louise or from my mother, lots of photos, and a couple of sentimental pieces of furniture. I thought I would miss all the books I had collected, but I don't."

Kind of makes you wonder what *your* stuff would be worth, doesn't it? Every time I move and look at the boxes around me, I get this urge to walk away from all of them.

If you ever feel trapped by your circumstances, think about what Jayne did. She reset by redefining. She could kill herself working in a soul-sucking job to pay for a place to keep her stuff, or she could stop needing so much stuff.

I have been fascinated by her life lesson and think it offers a great deal of comfort to those who find themselves stressed because of finances.

LESSEN YOUR CARES, INCREASE YOUR OPTIONS

As the bottom was falling out of the economy in 2008, I walked along the spectacular waterfront path on Edgewater Drive in Clearwater, Florida.

I wondered what the collapsed economy would do to the convention and meetings industry and, by extension, my income as a professional speaker for that industry. Might be pretty bad, I figured. A company that just laid off 10,000 people was certainly not going to hold a big conference and bring in an expensive speaker to talk happy talk.

This could really hurt me, I thought.

Then I looked out at the waterfront and saw a man sitting on a sailboat that had been moored offshore for months. I wondered what it cost that guy to live. Nothing, really. Food, a car if he has one onshore, gas for his dinghy, insurance, if he has it. That's about it.

And there he sat, blissfully soaking in the sun on a spectacular day, reading a book and appearing like he didn't have a single care in the world.

I literally started laughing to myself. Who was smarter? That guy was living a pretty good life!

I'd just seen how Jayne had liberated herself from her belongings, but watching that guy on his boat gave me *my* moment of liberation because it taught me that there are so many other options. That guy was probably spending less than $500 a month, and he was living way larger than I was.

There is no sin in passionately working hard or enjoying the nice things that money can buy. If you have purpose and meaning in your life, you are on the right path. But if you are trapped in a stress-filled existence with questionable reward, make changes. You may not have the luxury of making the professional change that will immediately free you from the bondage of a toxic work environment. But you do have the luxury of investing your spare time in the people you love and your spare brain cells doing things that matter.

When Wendy Kissinger was thirty-seven, she resigned from her executive job as employee relations director for the health system at the University of Florida in Gainesville. She took a fifty percent pay cut so she could work three days a week in a non-management position there as a development coordinator. The other four days a week were spent in St. Augustine, Florida, where she'd bought a tiny beach house for $75,000. She updated and remodeled it, then started singing and playing the guitar at local gigs to supplement her income.

Her older brother was thirty-seven when he was

killed in a car accident. When she reached that age, she knew how precious time was.

"Life is too short. I quit, and I never looked back," she said.

Wendy is amazing with money. Seven years before she went part-time, she tripled and quadrupled her mortgage payments until she paid off her house early. That gave her options. She's still setting aside a "healthy chunk" of her part-time income for savings.

"Less really is more," she said. "The less stuff I have, the less stress I have and the happier I am."

And she *is* happy. We did our interview as she was hostel-hopping with her backpack through Ireland. Not a bad life for a woman now in her early 50s.

LESS MONEY MEANS MORE LIFE

I met Helene Brien and Luc Parent at sunrise over Horseshoe Canyon near Moab, Utah. The French-Canadian couple retired in their fifties — ten years earlier than they planned. They sold their home, downsizing into a fifth wheel trailer, and then the passionate nature pho-tographers hit the road. They were starting their new life by spending a year traveling throughout the United States.

"I decided less money means more life," Luc told me.

I was so moved by what he said, I logged it in my iPhone.

Need less, live more.

I have been following their adventure on Facebook, mesmerized by their photographs. They are filling their lives with so much living. I sent a note telling them I wanted to share their story, and Luc shared something else that is just as potent.

"Someone explained to me that, if after one year of work, you are at the same point budget-wise and you did not make any change in your life, you've lost a year. It made me think, and it made me decide to make changes."

So status quo is a net loss.

Plenty of people work so hard just to maintain their current standard of living that they have little time to live large.

Helene said her early retirement cut her annual income in half for the ten years she could have continued working. But what if she'd waited? She thought a lot about it. If she delayed her big adventure, would she have had the health and vitality to dive into her dreams?

"My answer was no," she said. "It is now that I have the energy and opportunity to enjoy this, and this will allow me to have lasting memories for the rest of my life."

I'm fascinated by those who choose to cut back their standard of living in order to expand their quality of living.

I loved this Facebook post by P.J. Tedrick, a respiratory therapist who was getting ready to check out of the workforce at age 64. "To all those who say, 'But if you work longer you'll get more Social Security!' I respond thusly: I can get more money; I can't get more time," P.J. wrote. "I've taken care of hundreds of people who waited too long to retire, then never got to or had to do all those fun things alone because their spouse got sick or broke a hip, or, or, or . . . I'm not gonna do that.

"If I hafta go back to work later, I can learn to say, 'Welcome to Walmart' right along with the best of 'em.

But while I'm standing by the buggies, I'll be remembering the walks in the Mexican moonlight, the treks up the pyramids in Ecuador, the moon on the river in Croatia, the sun on the English castles . . . 'Hello there! Welcome to Wal-Mart!'"

I asked her about her post. Like Jayne, she'd realized she'd lived a life too caught up in "stuff."

"How much is enough? How many chairs do you need? You can only put your ass in one chair at a time! I've never been about amassing money. It's about freedom and seeing and experiencing other cultures. I didn't learn Spanish so I could plant myself like a petunia in the US and rot."

She has always been a hard worker and a good saver.

"I've always believed that you earn money so you can spend it doing the things that make you happy, and so you can help those who need it. Money just for the sake of a big bucketful is silly. You can't eat it. You can't plant it. You can't wear it or talk to it. It's simply a facilitator for all the important stuff."

Her work has really made the "live now, not later" theme come to life.

"I'm most aware of the blindsiding life can commit on people while they are sitting quietly, making plans to be fabulous. BAM! How about a heart attack? BOOM! How about a stroke? BOP! How about a car wreck?"

She is so right.

My mother suffered a paralyzing stroke at age 66. She and my dad never got the retirement of their dreams. Not one day of it. She required constant care, and when my dad was not working as a pharmacist (which he did until he was eighty-four), he was taking care of his beloved. It was backbreaking work that he said was his honor, but believe me, those two deserved some of the freedom and wonder that P.J. and Luc and Helene and Jayne are experiencing.

"We don't own a house," P.J. said. "We rent. I don't want to own anything anymore. We're selling our car, all our household stuff, and whatever will fit into a carry-on bag is what we'll own. We have a storage shed for grandma's quilts, pictures of the kids, mementos, and the novel nobody wanted to publish, but other than that, I am done with 'stuff.'"

There's that word again: STUFF.

"I got tired years ago of supporting my stuff. I rented/owned a house to house my stuff. I paid astronomical electric bills to air condition my stuff. I paid out the patoot to insure my stuff so that, if someone stole my stuff (which happened once), I could replace my stuff. Eventually, I figured I'd just get rid of the stuff and use the money to have fun. So that's what we did."

Your options are greater when you own your stuff, instead of your stuff owning you.

Financial worries are powerful barriers to many resets because they launch endless loops of negative or status quo thoughts like *I can't, I shouldn't,* or *I don't dare.* After all, you've got a future to worry about. But the stories I've just shared show how money frames our perspective and controls our behavior in ways we don't have to accept.

I had lunch yesterday with a woman who melted into tears as we talked about the pressure she feels being the primary breadwinner. The man she loves suffers from mental illness and may or may not be a continuing contributor to the household income. She's over her job, but stuck. She needs that big paycheck, even though she has to travel all the time and do work that no longer speaks to her soul.

I started asking her about expenses. At $3,500, her mortgage payment is two and a half times the average mortgage payment in her city. I can understand wanting a nice place, but living that large has shackled her. I told her to downsize. The pressure would immediately lift, and then, if she still hated her job, she could do something else.

But she can't let go.

She needs a financial reset so that she can then perform a lifestyle reset.

Once you have the confidence and the knowledge that you *can* survive on less, you can make decisions that let you live more. That doesn't necessarily mean you hold the biggest garage sale in history and get rid of your house and everything in it. It means you open your mind to defining success in ways that reflect the kind of activity and life you want.

Doing that means you have to get a handle on spending and debt. Do you realize that nearly eight out of ten Americans are living paycheck to paycheck? A 2013 survey by Bankrate.com reported that — and also found that those same people have little or no emergency savings. So if you're going to free your spirit, you have to first get beyond the money issues that are keeping you in shackles.

Forgive me if you don't need this advice from Tori Lewis, an accountant and certified financial planner. I realize that many people reading this book are more than financially secure. But many of you are not.

"I have a couple come in who make more than $200,000," she said. "One has a Lexus, one has a Beamer. They have nice watches and fancy briefcases. But they are so stressed out because they are in debt up to their eyeballs. They don't even sit next to each other. They made $11 in interest one year.

"Then I have a family of four that has only one wage earner making $30,000 a year. Their house is paid off.

"It's not what you make. It's what you don't spend."

And while everyone should have learned all of this in middle school, many people didn't. So I figured I'd welcome you all to the Tori Lewis School of Money.

"Do you know the best way to double your money?" she asked, reciting a famous line. "Fold it in half and put it back in your pocket."

Ahh.

Always save a windfall, she said. Every time. When her boyfriend won $107 at Bunko, she went home and wrote a check for $107 to his Roth IRA.

At least save half of a windfall, she said. Save half of the tax return. When you get a raise, bump up your contribution to your 401k.

"Every time you pay off a debt, increase your savings by that much," she said.

You'll be set for life.

If you have significant debt, it will take time to work your way out of it. But *start*. "With credit card debt, pay the minimum charge plus the interest plus any new purchases every month. It'll go down. And quit using credit cards."

Be careful with your debit card because "When you swipe, you don't think about how much you're spending."

Where did she get that discipline?

Two years into her college program, she ran out of money and went to her parents to ask for a loan.

"They said, 'We'll go talk about it.' They went into the bedroom for an hour and a half and came out and said, 'Yes. We will lend you $25.' That is a true story. I was crushed," she recalled.

So Tori quit her ten-hour a week job at McDonalds, where she was getting paid $4 an hour, then got a thirty-hour-a-week job waiting tables.

"You know what happened?" she asked. "My grades improved. And I actually graduated $2,000 ahead with no loans. It was tough love, and in that, my parents gave me the greatest gift of all: self-sufficiency. If they'd have been nicer to me, I'd have been a mooch like all those other kids.

"Money in the bank is the softest pillow you can lay your head on at night," she said.

It does give you more freedom.

Freedom to spend your time the way you want to spend it.

LESS IS MORE

"Too many people spend money they haven't earned, to buy things they don't want, to impress people they don't like."

— *Will Rogers*

"Life is really simple, but we insist on making it complicated."

— *Confucius*

LESS IS MORE

"There are two ways to be rich: One is by acquiring
much, and the other is by desiring little."

— *Author Jackie French Koller*

"Fear less, hope more; eat less, chew more;
whine less, breathe more; talk less, say more;
love more, and all good things will be yours."

— *Swedish proverb*

"The secret of happiness, you see, is not found
in seeking more, but in developing the
capacity to enjoy less."

— *Socrates*

"When you are content to be simply yourself
and don't compare or compete,
everybody will respect you."

— *Lao Tzu (philosopher and poet of ancient China)*

Plan for your future. Make it secure. But do not immerse yourself in a life that trades a vibrant present for a future that may or may not manifest. You don't want to be eating cat food in your retirement, but you don't have to eat caviar, either. Perhaps tuna will suffice if it means you can travel and have a few more years of fun.

Enjoy your life right NOW.

I have a friend who is a thirty-four-year-old veterinarian working six days a week, at least twelve hours a day. She's making great money, but her life sucks. Totally. Because she has no life. No relationship. No adventure. Nothing.

I looked her in the eyes and said, "Stop it. Really, stop it. The thirties are a lot like the twenties because you're young and everything is still in front of you. In a very short time, you will wake up and be forty. Now, forty is more connected to fifty than it is to thirty. You realize you're probably about halfway down the road. Gettin' to the other side. You still have an amazing time, but you are not a young person anymore. You're an adult. No denying it. You should be diving into your youth while you still have it."

She wants more, but she's working in such a demanding clinic that she can't have it. Choices. She could still do the work she loves, but in a place where she makes a *good* living, not a spectacular living. And then she could live more. But again, it's a choice.

"I'm used to this income," she said.

"But that income means you have no life," I shot back.

"Well, ya got me there." She smiled.

Do *you* have a life?

Is it as big and as meaningful and as fun as you want it to be?

If not, *why not?*

CHAPTER 20

RESETTING YOUR BOUNDARIES

When I turned fifty, I realized that much of the anxiety I'd experienced in life was because I was avoiding uncomfortable conversations. I'd rather put up with something awful, sometimes for years, than have an uncomfortable conversation.

Then a life-changing reality hit me: An uncomfortable conversation takes between three and fifteen minutes. Why spend years being miserable about something when you can set boundaries, have a short, uncomfortable conversation, and get rid of the problem?

How many uncomfortable conversations have you been avoiding? Is avoiding the problem worth it in the end?

There are always times we have to do things we don't want to do. We have to make appearances we don't want to make. We network with people we might not like. We work late and prioritize things that aren't our real priorities because we don't always have the luxury of throwing a tantrum and saying, "I'm not going to do that!"

But we throw away much more power than we actually use. Often, we are held back by fear or guilt.

If you are resetting your life, reset your boundaries.

I know a woman who has mastered the art of Southern hospitality too well and has an endless stream of company and moochers. Many of those people come empty-handed, expecting an all-inclusive resort from this woman who will buy groceries and alcohol, cook for them, and pour their wine. And she can't afford it all — not living on her Social Security income.

She could not get the word "No" to come out of her mouth because she didn't want to disappoint anybody.

But she's in her mid-seventies, and she loves her solitude. So why is she sacrificing the healthy years she has left exhausting herself to entertain so many people? Especially when so many of the people who come to enjoy her hospitality are people she's not even close to? On one occasion, someone was bringing a friend — for a whole week — and my friend was sick about it.

I gave her my lecture on uncomfortable conversations.

"Just have the uncomfortable conversation," I told her. "You will only be uncomfortable for fifteen minutes, and you will save yourself weeks of misery every year."

She never seemed to be able to get the words past her lips. For weeks, I kept coaching her to set a boundary, but she kept saying, "I can't do it."

Then I got the best call one morning.

"I did it!" she squealed. "I had my uncomfortable conversation!"

"See?" I said. "And it only took fifteen minutes, right?"

"It didn't take fifteen minutes," she said. "More like fifteen *seconds!*"

She could have started having conversations like that decades ago but she was too worried about making others uncomfortable. Instead, she made herself miserable.

Boundaries!

If you are being trampled over, get out of the way. Make changes. If you aren't naturally courageous, you have to train yourself to know what you want, honor that, then hold your breath and have a few uncomfortable conversations.

Yes, uncomfortable conversations *are* uncomfortable! They're not fun. But setting boundaries and honoring your true feelings is exhilarating. And the more you do it, the better you get at it. I've actually gotten quite comfortable with uncomfortable conversations.

YOU HAVE THE POWER

You can believe me, or you can waste years of doing things you don't want to do. You have the power. It's totally up to you.

Dorothy traveled the hard path down the Yellow Brick Road. Do you really want to do it the hard way?

Think of all Dorothy went through to find her power: munchkins, Scarecrow, Tin Man, Cowardly Lion, yellow brick road, nasty old wicked witch, and flying monkeys. All this to get to Oz, the place where the Great Wizard would fix everything. As we all know, the wizard was a total nincompoop, and somehow, Dorothy's getting back to Kansas depended on him haphazardly piloting a balloon back to Auntie Em. Toto jumped out of the balloon, Dorothy went after him, and the wizard took off without her.

The wizard shouted, "I can't come back! I don't know how it works!"

There was no hope.

But wait!

A bubble flew in from the distance, and who do we see but Glinda, the Good Witch of the South.

"You don't need to be helped any longer. You've always had the power to go back to Kansas," she told Dorothy.

"I have?" Dorothy asked.

"Then why didn't you tell her before?" Scarecrow asked.

And then Glinda said, "Because she wouldn't have believed me. She had to learn it for herself." Glinda continued, "Those ruby slippers you're wearing? Those are magic slippers that will take you home in two seconds!"

All Dorothy had to do was tap her heels together three times and repeat, "There's no place like home." Poof! She was home.

She'd had the power the whole time, but she had to learn her lesson the hard way.

So you can live your life the hard way, or you can remember this: You have so much power. It's always there, right inside of you.

Stand your ground. Set boundaries. Stop settling. Have those uncomfortable conversations.

You have the power!

You've always had the power.

CHAPTER 21

RESETTING YOUR AGE

At least a decade ago, I saw a woman who looked to be about eighty years old whipping through traffic in a classic orange Corvette convertible. The only thing she didn't do was squeal out when the light changed.

But that woman looked ready to rumble.

I wanted to follow her home and get her story. I wanted to learn from her because the smile on her face said everything. Nothing was going to slow her down. Nothing. Certainly not her age.

The memory of her brazen moment behind the wheel of that convertible continues to inspire me.

Some people just endure life.

Some people choose to live life.

And some people choose to *really* live life.

You need to make the choice to really live your life.

It's your adventure.

It took a while for me to understand how to do this for myself.

The first time I felt old was on New Year's Eve, 1989. I was twenty-nine years old.

Twenty-nine, and I felt old!

My then-husband and friends had conked out by 11

p.m. after a long day of skiing, and I sat there in the Steamboat Springs, Colorado condo watching the ball drop in Times Square on television — all by myself.

The party was over.

That was my life.

We were officially old.

I popped the champagne cork, then walked out into the cold where I raised my glass to the sky and said, "Next year, I will be a year younger."

That was my resolution. Instead of resigning myself to living a life of ruts and predictability, I would keep shaking things up, refusing to settle down and be boring.

The year that followed was a great year. I did my first Ride the Rockies, a 430-mile, seven-day cycling adventure in the mountains. I hiked many miles. And when New Year's rolled around again, I was on the Champs-Élysées in Paris.

It's kind of silly, a twenty-nine-year-old feeling "old," because a twenty-nine-year-old is, in so many ways, still a little chick who doesn't yet know how to cluck. But I honor that memory because that was my truth in that moment. I *was* an old lady. I hadn't learned to celebrate my youth.

I was married.

I was in a routine.

I knew what tomorrow was going to be like. And the next day.

When you always know what's coming, and what's coming isn't very exciting, you are in a rut. You either choose to remain in that rut, or you can climb out of it. But don't blame your rut for making you miserable. You have the power to make changes.

AGE VS. AGING

You can't control your age, but you can definitely control how old you are. Age and aging are two very different things. There is no stopping the aging process, although many of us try to fight our wrinkles or control our longevity with exercise and diet and a little cosmetic help.

But age? Age is a number. You know people who are old in years but don't seem old at all. And you know people who are young in years but seem utterly ancient. You can stop growing old the minute you decide you are going to be one of the cool people who lives young.

I still remember when Sue Lindsay, one of my fellow reporters, celebrated her fortieth birthday by buying her first Harley. That was the same year that I was twenty-nine and feeling like an old lady. Forty seemed ancient at the time, but now it seems mighty young. Everything becomes oh-so-relative.

I loved the bravado that came with Sue's gesture of getting a bad-ass motorcycle right at one of those turning-point birthdays when the "over the hill" jokes start getting louder. She'd wear the bad-ass clothes and exude cool. She was so much older than I was, but I knew then that she was so much younger.

Then — get this — she had a baby at age forty-four.

Fearless.

I remember what my dad said to me on his eightieth birthday.

"I'm not sure how this happened," he said. "I'm eighty years old. Eighty years old!"

Eighty years old on the outside, but he felt forty — or even thirty — on the inside. I get it.

The fact that time passes so quickly leaves a lot of us bewildered.

My friend Denise told me that no one will talk to her at work.

"Why?" I asked.

"Because I'm the old person," she said.

I was astonished. She is a strikingly beautiful fifty-eight-year-old who could pass for ten years younger any day. And no one will talk to her? It's like there's something wrong with her because of her age!

How sad that some people automatically cast older people out or treat them as if they are invisible — especially since time will move so fast that the young whippersnappers will soon be perceived as invisible, too.

I live large because I know I will never be as young as I am right now. I'd better enjoy this minute for all the possibility it holds. It's going to end. Things are going to change. And quickly.

The day will come when I hit my eightieth birthday and think of my dad. I'll wonder how that happened to *me*, too. I'm making certain that I put as much life in my years as I can.

The challenge is for all of us to find out what keeps us active, viable, and cool, whether we're contemplating feeling old in our twenties or our eighties. The only people I've seen get old are the ones who gave up on being young. Granted, many times the surrender comes because of health problems that interfere with and diminish the quality of life. But until you have those kinds of problems, you might as well drink in all the life that you can.

When I catch myself missing a beautiful day because

I'm consumed by my work or too lazy to get out and exercise, I kick myself in the butt and get out there. I am not getting this day back. I am either going to live it large or miss the whole moment.

I can either force myself to finish writing this whole chapter before I have a little fun, or I can go have a little fun and then write the chapter. You can bet I am about to log out right now because the sun is shining, and I want to walk the beach. I want to walk the beach because I *can* walk the beach. My legs are strong. I'm healthy. Why wouldn't I enjoy this beautiful day?

We are not afforded an endless supply of beautiful days and good health with which to enjoy them. So we must get out there while the gettin' is good.

Nobody is going to kick you in the butt and tell you to get moving. You have to do that for yourself.

EVERYTHING IS RELATIVE.

A seven-year-old thinks a fifteen-year-old is a grown-up. A twenty-five-year-old sees a forty-five-year-old as someone their parents' age. An eighty-year-old sees a forty-five-year-old as a young person. No matter how old you are, you are either young or old to somebody else.

Learn to define your age without thinking of the categories others try to put you into. It's very easy to always feel old, but it's a much greater challenge to always feel young. Age shows up in our slow-moving bones, our grey hairs, and our wrinkled skin. We are reminded of it every time we fill out any sort of survey that requires us to check a box indicating our age range. Usually, the boxes stop at "sixty-five or older," as if it's a category of leftovers.

It's ironic that, at sixty-five, we are finally afforded the freedom to do what we want and play full time, like kids liberated by the school bell for summer break.

Linda Brown is my hero. She is seventy-eight, and right now she is somewhere in Uruguay. I think. I never know because Linda's been living out of a backpack and traveling the world for years. She'll leave for a year at a time. Sometimes longer. Then she'll breeze back into town for a couple of weeks as she figures out where she's going next.

She does all of this by herself, living on her monthly Social Security payout and a little bit of savings. She stays in hostels and has about a million friends of all ages all over the world. People are mesmerized by her.

She's taught me so much, and I listen when she says, "Age is a number, just a number, and I choose not to pay attention to it."

Instead of fretting about what is to come, she's sucking every bit of life out of every single moment. I get e-mails from her telling her tales about doing some of the most exciting — and sometimes the most hair-brained — things you could imagine, but every update is a thrill. She travels between countries faster than most people venture between counties. Nothing will stop her.

She is fearless. She is alive.

Emilia Vergara is our oldest living, performing mermaid. She started doing shows in Florida's Weeki Wachee Springs back in 1957. She took a time-out after she got married and had kids but returned to the springs in the 1990s to perform as one of the "Legendary Sirens."

She lights up when she talks of performing or training with the other mermaids. In that water, it's 1957 again, and she is a stunning young mermaid. She has taught me so much about defining life with passion and motion. I've seen her climb a tree and swing from a rope, letting out a Tarzan yell as she drops to the river below her. She and I once hiked in a rainforest and spontaneously jumped into a waterfall.

She's not old. Not at all.

DO WHAT MAKES YOU FEEL YOUNG

There's a saying that goes "You don't stop exercising because you get old, you get old because you stop exercising." There is so much truth to that. People who fill their lives with activity and movement are happier, stronger, and more fulfilled.

What makes you feel young? Embrace it. For me, it comes when I feel the sand between my toes at the beach. Or when I'm kayaking at sunset. Or when I take a sunset swim off Honeymoon Island. There is always some sort of physical interaction with my world that makes me feel alive.

Some people age without getting old. Don't resign yourself to a rut because *that* is what getting old is all about. Fill your life with excitement and adventure, with people and energy. Don't give up on the possibility that still exists in every single moment of every single day.

You do not have the power to stop the clock. You are aging every minute, and you are definitely going to get older. But whether or not you choose to actually *be* old is up to you. That doesn't mean you have to dress in revealing, teenage clothing, play loud music, and buy a flashy sports car that just isn't you. But don't stop having fun just because other people around you have surrendered their youth to the aging process and stopped pushing their limits and growing.

Don't bow to the expectations of others that, since you are aging, you should be less than you once were.

Be more.

If you have had a few of those moments when you wonder about the meaning of life, stop wondering and start living it. Instead of asking "Is this all there is?" shake things up until you're saying, "I never knew I could have this much fun!" Don't wonder what your life has added up to — take steps to make it add up to more every day.

The day is coming when you won't have the physical agility to do what you want to do. Are you using your good years the best way you can while you don't have so many limits? Or are you frittering away your time by unconsciously giving in to routines and ruts, wasting your time doing things you do not enjoy and things that don't fulfill you?

I am going to repeat this over and over again.

You get one life. There is no do-over. This is it. What you have today may not be available to you tomorrow. If you don't do what matters to you now, you might not ever get the chance to do it.

If you are not living the life that fulfills you, gives you purpose, and defines you with meaning, *WHAT ARE YOU WAITING FOR?*

Certain aspects of aging really suck. You aren't as strong or as fast or as vibrant as you used to be. You look in the mirror and wonder who the hell that old person is. You're looking like Mom or Dad or Granny or Gramps. Your bones ache. You need surgeries.

But what's the alternative?

At which age would you like to stop progressing? Twenty? Thirty? Forty? You've already had those experiences, good and bad. Do you really want to stop the clock and stay there, or do you want to keep growing and learning?

Aging isn't a bad thing. It forces us to learn. We aren't here on this earth to discover the one thing that works, and then do it over and over and over again with the same results. By aging — and changing physically, emotionally, spiritually, professionally, personally — we are forced to re-invent, learn, and discover new facets of ourselves.

YOU MATTER

It may not be pretty, but aging is the opportunity to go deep and continue going deeper. It would be impossible to experience our full soul growth if we stayed the same age.

Granted, it's unnerving. Time seems to move faster every year. But we are really moving at the same speed at which we have always moved. It just seems faster because we keep looking in the mirror and seeing changes we don't necessarily like, changes that show us moving closer to the end of our time here. It's painful because we no longer just sense our mortality, we *see* it. It's personal.

So you can resent it or open yourself up. Go deep. Then, go deeper. Learn as you grow older. When you start to feel like you're becoming obsolete, remember that you are just graduating into another classroom.

So you look in the mirror and see someone far older than you feel like you are. It makes you mad. You feel like people don't hear you as well, that they are slower to engage with you, and that they are quicker to dismiss you. Stop worrying. You have faced more learning moments than they have. Just keep living and learning until you graduate out of here.

Instead of fighting your age, groove with it. Instead of acting your age, redefine it. You can be the old bag who complains about everything, or the sassy one who makes everybody laugh. Go buy your orange Corvette convertible. Race it real loud. Don't hold back.

Yes, you may have some wrinkles, and maybe you've got the dreaded turkey neck. But you are wiser, and you matter.

Remember that.

You matter.

As much as you ever mattered, and maybe even more.

CHAPTER 22
RESETTING YOUR PAST

It's hard to move forward when you are stuck in your past.

Life will give you plenty of adversity, and life wounds take time to heal. Wear your wounds, but don't wear them for too long.

Every time you ruminate on the things that didn't go right, every time you use it as a "yeah, but ..." or as an excuse for not thriving, and every time you talk about what happened, you give your pain new life. When you have been victimized or wronged, it is often so hard to let go and move on. But who are you punishing when you don't? How much of your happiness are you willing to sacrifice because of something you can't do anything about?

"If you want to get over a problem, stop talking about it. Your mind affects your mouth, and your mouth affects your mind." What a great truth from Joyce Meyer.

You relive your victimization or misfortune every time you tell the story. Talking about it gives it life. Of course, you have to do the initial processing, but there comes a time when you need to shut up about it and stop fixating on it. If you got dumped, stop checking that person's Facebook page. Stop asking about the person, and stop telling your story of woe. How does that help you?

Don't forget to reset your past. Don't fall into the trap of holding on to something you shouldn't hold on to.

I know a woman who divorced twenty years ago and is still bitterly recounting every detail of how her husband ruined her life. He may have ruined their marriage, but that was twenty years ago! She is the one who ruined her life. By not letting go, she stayed stuck in her anger, abandonment, and fear.

I have a coaching client who was fired a decade ago by a boss who could easily have been certified as a lunatic. She couldn't let go of it. She felt it defined her as a failure, even though what happened truly wasn't her fault. Stuck in that negativity, she could not perform to the best of her ability. It was a growth moment that took her a dozen years to grow out of.

Think of the people you know who never really rebound after a loss of a relationship, loved one, position, or dream. Don't be one of them.

Your past gave you your great moments of learning. Instead of being permanently scarred by the especially hard lessons, let yourself be empowered by the learning that occurred in spite of what may have been some very bad obstacles or choices. Instead of reliving hardships, failures, and losses that may have hurt and scarred you, take the understanding and wisdom that you gained and move on.

The past is just a thought, anyhow. It's a memory, a perception, an interpretation. There is nothing solid about it except what you keep of it in your mind. The past is a vibration — a recollection — and the only way it can exist is if you give it more power and energy than it actually has. Everybody does it. Your past either exists or doesn't exist based on whether the memories are given energy.

It's interesting that I say that, given that this whole book was predicated on the darkest moment in my life. But, aside from sharing my growth moments as a lesson for others, I'm not dwelling on what happened because it is in my past. I can't change it. The final step of healing occurs when you say, "It's time to move on."

One of the greatest achievements in life is learning to control the thoughts that make you happy or sad. Perhaps you have happy memories in your past that you wish to keep close to you. Enjoy those memories, but see them for what they are: good memories.

Your past is a memory. It's a moment of learning. If you keep reliving it, you're stuck in the ether rather than moving forward with your current moment, which is a fresh opportunity for you to define.

Some people hold grudges based upon emotion based on something that happened to them in the past. Other people do not. What's a grudge except an emotion that can either exist or not exist? Why would you choose to have one if you can choose not to have one?

BE IN THE PRESENT

The only moment that's truly your reality is the one you are experiencing right now. That is the only moment that really exists, and you lose it by looking back or looking ahead. Right now is the moment you need to fill with light and love and life. How are you going to live it? Are you going to continue through your life stuck in something that no longer exists? Because the past is there in your mind, but it's gone from reality in the here and now. It can be big for you or it can be nothing at all.

The past is simply training for the present. It shapes who you have become, but it does not decide who you will be — unless you allow it to do so. When you focus on what's new and present, you can overwrite so many of the negatives you experienced in your past — but it takes a great deal of inner discipline to intentionally do this. It takes a lot of forgiveness, of yourself and others. It takes perspective to use all of the things that have happened around you — good or bad — to make you a better you in this moment.

FORGIVENESS

One of the biggest roadblocks to letting go of the past and moving forward is forgiveness. If you want to be forgiven for your past mistakes, big or small, you have to be willing to extend forgiveness to others. If you want to be able to move on from the things you did not handle well, forgive others for the things they did not handle well. If you don't want someone to relish your difficulties, don't relish theirs.

"Forgive others, not because they deserve forgiveness, but because you deserve peace."
— *Author Jonathan Lockwood Huie*

"Forgiveness is me giving up my right to hurt you for hurting me."
— *Anonymous*

"The past cannot be changed, forgotten, edited, or erased; it can only be accepted."
— *Anonymous*

When we are victimized, we naturally want to see our victimizer suffer some sort of retribution, and sometimes it feels good to watch the person who hurt us take a fall. We want to see justice served — it's only natural. But by waiting for it, we continue to attach ourselves to our victimization. Ultimately, justice can and will be served.

We are learning to be better human beings. We have so many chances to deepen ourselves. Some people take the path, and some don't. If the people who have wronged you find a way to be better, don't resent them for not learning those lessons before they dealt with you — just feel gratitude that they got the lesson at all. Remember that you didn't get some of your life lessons in time to prevent hurting others, either.

It all comes down to forgiveness — forgiving others and forgiving yourself. That's where a true reset occurs. Because once you let go, you grow.

"Forgiveness is a gift you give to yourself." I heard that quote years ago, and now everyone from Suzanne Somers to Tony Robbins is claiming it. Since everyone is claiming the words, you might as well do it, too. Hang onto them, because they so succinctly sum up the "why" of forgiveness. It isn't about the other person. It's about you. Every anger, misgiving, or resentment you cling to hurts *you*, not the person who wronged you.

Once you let go of it for yourself, you can often take the step of forgiving in total. You can then forgive the other person for his or her sake.

My ex-husband and I talk almost every week, and we've been divorced for more than twenty years. There were some deep hurts that led to our split, but if I'd hung onto them, I would have completely lost someone I loved. My life would be emptier without him. So he has my complete forgiveness — and believe me, I'm sure he has had to do some forgiving, too.

Why choose animosity and resentment when you can let go, move on, and rebuild something new and different?

You can forgive someone that you never want to see again. I've done that. It comes down to a question of how much you want to let that person re-victimize you in absentia. Do you think that client's former boss would have felt bad about having scarred that woman for so many years? Pretty doubtful. So who was she punishing?

Have you been punishing yourself by getting stuck in the past? Let go. Move on.

C. S. Lewis summed it up best: "Getting over a painful experience is much like crossing monkey bars. You have to let go at some point in order to move forward."

CONCLUSION

I started this book comparing our life resets to a computer reboot. The computer gets sluggish, it isn't working right, and you reset. Voila! Just like that, it's refreshed. It's alive. It's like new. I told you that you have the ability to do that for yourself.

Well, in conclusion, let there be a conclusion.

Once you have reset, close the book and move on. Let your new day be a new day.

After my beach walk, I started showing a three-minute video to my audiences, sharing the magic of my reset. The video showed my sandy white beaches, the sun, the waves, the dolphins, and the splendor of growing and moving into my power. People told me how inspiring it was, and the video always got huge applause.

"This is the last time I will show this video," I told the leadership conference at Deloitte. It was the one-year anniversary of my beach walk. I was in the same venue I'd been one year earlier when I'd had that dark moment that had cried out for the reset.

The video hadn't lost its power.

But the time had come for me to close the book on my experience.

The final stage of reset is its conclusion.

It's the realization that you've made changes for

yourself and are ready to internalize the learning you received and move on.

Whether you're resetting your view of your past, your relationships, your direction, your career focus, your work-life balance, your boundaries, or anything else that needs a fresh start, there comes a point when you have to wrap it up and let yourself fully reset.

You don't forget where you came from — that's your history and that's what brought you to this point. But you don't have to relive it over and over again.

It's a new day, so why spend energy reliving an old one?

You've reset.

MEET THE AUTHOR

FAWN GERMER will reach inside of you and pull out your best self by showing you how to get beyond the self-limiting behaviors that hold so many of us back. She once had a boss tell her that she'd never be more than she was at the time — a reporter — and she sure showed him. Fawn is a four-time Pulitzer-nominated investigative journalist and the author of eight books, including the Oprah pick *Hard Won Wisdom.*

Fawn interviewed more than 300 of the most accomplished leaders of our times, including US Presidents, Olympic athletes, CEOs, prime ministers, Academy Award winners, and many other trailblazers who shared with her the secrets of true success.

From them, she learned that success is born out of risk, and power comes from a self-awareness that disables the issues of doubt and self-esteem.

Her first book was rejected by every major publisher in the United States, but Fawn persevered until it was a bestseller. She wrote twenty-nine letters to Oprah, and something broke through, with Oprah ultimately holding up *Hard Won Wisdom* and telling the world how "very inspiring" Fawn's work was.

After that, Fawn became one of the most sought-after leadership and motivational speakers. She travels the globe with her message of viability, performance, and power. She has keynoted for Coca-Cola, Kraft, Ford Motor Company, Cisco, Pfizer, Hallmark, Deloitte, Kimberly Clark, Xerox, Bayer, AIG, Novartis, GlaxoSmithKline, the Network of Executive Women, Harvard, the UCLA Anderson School of Business, the Wharton School of Business, and many others.

Fawn is an avid kayaker, cyclist, and adventurer who lives in Dunedin, Florida.